Nonfiction Reading Power

Teaching students how to think while they read all kinds of information

Adrienne Gear

Stenhouse Publishers
PORTLAND, MAINE

Pembroke Publishers Limited
MARKHAM, ONTARIO

Dedication

To Spencer and Oliver, with love

Pembroke Publishers
538 Hood Road
Markham, Ontario, Canada L3R 3K9
www.pembrokepublishers.com

Published in the U.S. by Stenhouse Publishers
480 Congress Street
Portland, ME 04101
www.stenhouse.com

We acknowledge the financial support of the Government of Canada through
the Book Publishing Industry Development Program (BPIDP) for our
publishing activities.

We acknowledge the Government of Ontario through the Ontario Media
Development Corporation's Ontario Book Initiative.

Library and Archives Canada Cataloguing in Publication

Gear, Adrienne
   Nonfiction reading power : teaching students how to think while they read
all kinds of information / Adrienne Gear.

Includes index.
ISBN 978-1-55138-229-6

   1. Reading comprehension. 2. Reading (Elementary). I. Title.

LB1050.45.G42 2008   372.47   C2008-903754-5

Editor: Kat Mototsune
Cover Design: John Zehethofer
Typesetting: Jay Tee Graphics Ltd.

Printed and bound in Canada
9 8 7 6

MIX
Paper from
responsible sources
FSC
www.fsc.org   FSC® C004071

Contents

What Is Fiction?
(sung to the tune of "Frère Jacques")

What is fiction? What is fiction?
It's not true. It's not true!
Elephants are flying,
Polar bears are driving—
It's not true! It's not true!

Funny, scary; monster, fairy.
Adventure, too. Adventure, too!
Characters and setting,
Beginning and an ending—
But it's not true. It's not true!

What's nonfiction? What's nonfiction?
Is it true? Yes, it's true!
Facts and information
But not imagination
Because it's true. Yes, it's true!

Charts and labels, webs and tables.
Captions, too. Captions, too!
Frogs and bugs and habitats,
Planets, weather, whales, and bats
It's all true! Yes, it's TRUE!

Foreword

When I graduated from the University of British Columbia nearly 20 years ago, I was thrilled to be able to call myself a real teacher. Having spent the majority of my life up to that point learning in school, I assumed that I knew pretty much everything there was to know. Now, with many years of teaching behind me, I realize how little I actually knew that first year I stood proudly in front of my first class. I still consider myself a teacher, but first and foremost a learner. Since starting in this great profession, I have been on a continual learning journey. Yes, I may know a few things that my students don't know, but I continue to learn a great deal about what I do through working with students, though reading, through conversations with colleagues, through attending workshops and conferences, through reflecting on my work. When presenting workshops to teachers, my hope always is that they will not only leave with some practical ideas to use in their classrooms, but that they will have experienced a shift in their thinking about reading comprehension and traveled just a little further in their own learning journey. Writing this book is just my way of encouraging travel.

Seven years ago, I was given five minutes to present the importance of comprehension instruction to my colleagues during a staff meeting. I had recently read Stephanie Harvey and Anne Goudvis' book *Strategies That Work* and, based on some of the big ideas in this book, had come up with an idea of how we, as a staff, might begin to practically implement some of the key concepts into our literacy programs. Not only did I have to convince my colleagues why it is important that we all teach reading comprehension but, more importantly, I also needed to present how to do that in a way that would be viewed as manageable and practical. Had I passed out a list of eight or twelve strategies and told everyone that they needed to be teaching them, I don't imagine that there would have been too much "buy in" on the part of the staff. I therefore selected five strategies that I believed would be a starting place. Five seemed a reasonable number and breaking it down would mean focusing on one strategy approximately every two months. And so Reading Power was born.

A year after we began teaching the strategies using picture books, the question was raised: "What about nonfiction? Do we teach the same strategies when we are working with nonfiction texts?" I had to ask myself: Does my brain engage with nonfiction texts the same way it engages with fiction? Some strategies, such as asking questions, making connections, and inferring, may be ones that I use, but certainly there seemed to be other strategies that were necessary for making sense of nonfiction material that we had not focused on with the fiction texts. I went back to the original research and looked carefully at our provincial performance standards for reading for information. I noticed two strategies, which we had not focused on for reading fiction, that seemed to be predominant strategies for reading for information: helping students recognize and interpret nonfiction text features and conventions, and helping students learn to determine importance or the main idea of a piece.

The focus of this book is helping students find meaning in informational texts. *Nonfiction Reading Power* starts by outlining Reading Power as it is used in the classroom, the research upon which it is based, and its three main components: the model, the book lists, and the method of instruction. The chapters that follow provide some practical strategies for making sense of informational texts with a specific in-depth look into five strategies or "reading powers": Zoom-In, Question/Infer, Determine Importance, Connect, and Transform.

John A. Shedd (1928) once wrote, "A ship in the harbor is safe, but that is not what ships were built for." Like many teachers, I have a tendency to keep pulling out the tried and true units that have worked for me in the past. Even five years ago, it was easier to stay close to the harbor of my comfort zone than to venture out into the uncharted territory of nonfiction comprehension. Since then, however, it has found a permanent place on my teaching map. I encourage you to venture out into uncharted territories and to explore the amazing world of nonfiction with your students.

Enjoy your journey!

Adrienne Gear

Introduction

I grew up in a generation where the word "comprehension" was associated with comprehension questions: "Read this chapter, then answer the questions." Comprehension was something we did, not something we learned. The purpose of reading in school was to find the right answers. "And if you don't understand how to get the answers right, have no fear, just keep practicing! There will be plenty more opportunities for you to get the answers wrong!" In this situation, as in any learning situation, practice does NOT make perfect if no instruction on what "perfect" is has been provided. My teachers did not teach me how to make sense of what I was reading; as long as I could read the words, I was considered a reader.

Sadly, I brought this misguided notion of comprehension with me into my early teaching years and continued to "assign and assess" comprehension questions to my intermediate students. When students did not do well, I certainly felt badly, but I did what my own teachers had done—hand the questions back and ask them to do their corrections. I reflect on this absurd situation with a certain degree of embarrassment. What was I thinking? That, somehow, the second time around, the student would miraculously find the correct answers? Thankfully, research over the past twenty years has guided educators to the realization that comprehension is not something we "do" but something we "teach" and that explicit instruction in comprehension should precede independent practice.

Comprehension Research

For more than 20 years, educational research has looked at ways to try to determine what good readers do when they read. In his extensive study through the University of Michigan, P. David Pearson determined that proficient readers use specific strategies to make sense of what they are reading (Pearson & Gallagher, 1983). Over the past several years, this list of reading strategies has been slowly making its way into classrooms, as teachers become more aware of the importance of the explicit instruction in comprehension. These research-based strategies enable a reader to become more engaged and to interact with the text to find meaning. While many proficient readers use these strategies innately, or subconsciously, research points to a more conscious, or metacognitive, approach where readers learn to become more aware of their thinking and are able to "talk through the text." Equally as important as learning the strategy is developing the "language of thinking" to be able to articulate what strategy was used and how it helped with the comprehension of the text.

Strategies Used by Proficient Readers

A good reader is **metacognitive**—aware of and able to use and articulate the following strategies in order to interact with the text.

1. **Make Connections.** An active reader is able to draw from background knowledge and personal experiences while reading to help create meaning from the text.

2. **Ask Questions.** An active reader asks both literal and inferential questions before, during, and after reading to clarify and deepen understanding.

3. **Visualize.** An active reader is able to create multi-sensory images in the "mind's eye" while reading to help make sense of the text.

4. **Draw Inferences.** An active reader knows that not all information is included in a text, and is able to hypothesize and predict what is going to happen next, based on evidence in the text.

5. **Determine Importance.** An active reader sifts through information in the text to select important ideas, choose what to remember, and set priorities.

6. **Analyze and Synthesize.** An active reader is able to break down information and to draw conclusions based on both the text and his or her own thinking.

7. **Monitor Comprehension.** An active reader is aware when understanding is being compromised and is able to stop, go back, and reread in order for understanding to occur.

(Based on the research of P. David Pearson)

Research shows that, for very few students, the ability to comprehend is a natural result of decoding.

Many educators in the field of comprehension instruction, including Stephanie Harvey, Anne Goudvis, Debbie Miller, and Ellin Keene, have based much of their practice on David Pearson's research. Their work reflects the complexity of comprehension, and its being a separate, yet equally important, aspect of reading. "Reading demands a two-pronged attack. It involves cracking the alphabetic code to determine the words and thinking about those words to construct meaning" (Harvey & Goudvis 2000, p. 5). The graphic on page 11 breaks down reading into two main areas: Decoding and Comprehension. Teaching decoding strategies, generally speaking, is the focus of reading instruction in the primary grades. An enormous amount of instructional time is devoted to helping students learn letters, sounds, blends, word endings, how sounds are combined to make words, how words are combined to make sentences, etc. By the time students complete the primary grades, it is the general expectation that they have learned the skills and strategies that enable them to read the words on the page. But does the ability to decode equate being a reader? I know that many of us have had students in our classes who have developed into what I refer to as "the master decoder": students who are "reading" the words on the page, but who are not engaged with the text. What those students have missed along the way is an awareness that learning to read is not just about being able to say the words, but understanding what those words mean.

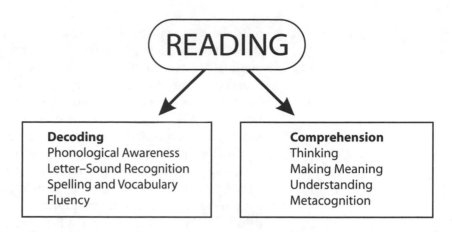

Comprehension is an equally important aspect of learning to read as decoding. Yet is there the same amount of instructional time being spent "teaching" comprehension as there is teaching decoding? For many of us, the answer is no. But if learning to read requires both the ability to say what's on the page and to understand what those words say, then surely we need to provide our students with a balance of instruction in both. Reading Power focuses specifically on how we can teach students what comprehension is and how they can become better engaged to find meaning within the texts they read.

When my eldest son was in Grade 2, I received the call from the school in late fall: "Adrienne, we have some concerns about Spencer's reading." For any parent who has been on the receiving end of such a call, you will know how difficult it is. (The fact that I am a Literacy Mentor in the school district didn't help the situation!) But it was no surprise to me that Spencer was labeled a "struggling reader," as I had listened to him "struggle" every night on the couch. Spencer was the opposite of the "master-decoder"; he struggled with code. Daily reading in our living room was a painful experience. At times I, too, fixated on the code, feeling his frustration when he sounded out a word unsuccessfully over and over, and suppressing my desire to shout "It says 'umbrella'! Now move on!" When I asked him to explain what he found the most difficult part of reading, he responded, "Mummy, I'm just not smooth."

For Spencer, the invitation into the text was a welcome relief. Despite the fact that decoding was a challenge for him, the realization that he could move away from the surface of the text and into his own thinking helped him to feel successful and to recognize that reading was not just about what was on the page, but also about what was in his head. The label "struggling reader," in my opinion, is not indicative of the Spencers of the world. He is a struggling decoder, but not a struggling thinker. Just as written output is not always a reflection of cognitive ability, the ability to decode is not always a reflection of the understanding. It is an important lesson, perhaps, for us all.

The World of Nonfiction : A Personal History

As a child, I loved to read. I devoured *Betsy and Billy*, the Little House books, *All of a Kind Family*, *Betsy, Tasey and Tibb*, *Charlotte's Web*, Enid Blyton, Roald Dahl, Astrid Lingren—books that I have heard on more than one occasion been referred to as "girly books." I remember the library in my elementary school—quiet and inviting on the side where the fiction books lined the shelves, filled baskets, and twirled around in those metal stands; sunlight streaming through the windows; the soft comfy couch and bright cushions. And when Mrs. Sterling, the teacher-librarian, did her book talk on the new books that would soon be appearing on the shelves and twirly gigs, I could hardly contain myself. Yet there was one part of the library that was not appealing to me: the Nonfiction side. In my memory, that section of the library had no windows, no cushions—just shelves and shelves of books that were too hard for me to read. Nonfiction, in my elementary-school mind, was a hard-covered book on the dark side of the library, one that described an insect, dinosaur, mammal, or ancient Egypt, with an occasional *Christmas Crafts for 3–5-Year-Olds* thrown in for good measure. Nonfiction was information found in a dark dusty book or those dreaded volumes of Encyclopedia Britannica. It was, as I look back on it, literally and figuratively "the dark side" of the library; certainly not a place I frequented.

My Grade 3 teacher Mrs. LaPierre announced one day that we were about to embark on an "animal research project." She explained that we would be working in the library with Mrs. Sterling. I immediately began to feel a little uncomfortable, knowing that it would inevitably mean regular visits to "the dark side." Mrs. LaPierre then walked up and down the rows of desks holding up a purple velvet hat. One at a time, my classmates reached into this hat and pulled out a folded piece of white paper, revealing the name of the animal they would be researching. The anticipation grew as papers were unfolded and animal names were excitedly announced: Panda, Horse, Chipmunk, Leopard. All the animals drawn by the other children were cute, furry, exciting, or a combination thereof. The animal name I drew from the purple velvet hat was neither cute and furry, nor exciting. I sat silently staring at the letters on the white slip. The boy behind me peered over my shoulder and shouted, "Armadillo. What's that?!" Mrs. LaPierre explained that the beauty of research is that it enables you to find out about something that you knew nothing about. I did not wish to find out anything about the armadillo. Then the boy behind me whispered "Your animal's ugly." So I sat quietly in my desk and began to cry.

Flash ahead 20 years to my own Grade 4 classroom. Picture books and novels are displayed on shelves and window sills, posters of Newbery Award-winning books are displayed, a cozy reading corner is situated under the windows, with cushions and a couch. I even have my own metal twirly stand that I salvaged from a library reno. Fiction permeates every corner of my classroom. Nonfiction titles are scarce. They are crammed into one tub labeled *NONFICTION* that is not easily accessible. My daily read-alouds are from fiction texts: picture books or chapters from a novel. My spring author study is on an author of fiction: Kevin Henkes, Jez Alborough, Chris Van Allsburg. My daily reading activities revolve around the world of fiction.

Each year, as the end of second term approaches, I begin to feel the guilt of presenting an unbalanced program. I quickly visit my colleague and friend, Amy Wou, the teacher-librarian, and book some time for the much-anticipated unit: the Arctic Animal Research Report. Since we are studying the Inuit people, there is an obvious link to the animals of the polar region. I begin this exciting journey into the world of research similarly to Mrs. LaPierre: carefully writing the names of all the arctic animals (polar bear, Arctic fox, caribou, lemming) on little slips of white paper, folding the slips and placing them in an overturned baseball cap. With great enthusiasm, I announce to my Grade 4 class that we are about to embark on an exciting journey into the world of the researcher. Each child eagerly

"This notion of defining nonfiction too restrictively includes report writing, in particular animal reports, a favorite of thousands of teachers around the country. While it is true that these teachers are studying nonfiction, this type of report writing is only a fraction of what nonfiction texts are about."—Tony Stead (2002)

and excitedly draws their animal name from the hat. The child who chooses lemming looks slightly disappointed and a little confused.

"What's wrong?" I ask.

"I don't know what a lemming is."

"Well," I reply in my best Mrs. LaPierre voice, "that's the beauty of research. You will discover something new about something you knew nothing about." Off we troop to the library. All the Arctic animal books have been pulled from the shelves and are displayed on tables. Most are too difficult for my Grade 4 students to read. I have already pulled my file on animal research and made 28 copies of the legal-sized note-taking sheet with the five research headings: Description, Food, Enemies, Habitat, Interesting Facts. ("If you don't know where to put something, just write it in Interesting Facts.")

The students spend the next few weeks learning to take notes about their animal. I do remember teaching note-taking skills. I do not, however, recall teaching them anything about reading and understanding the text features, finding the main idea, connecting to background knowledge, etc. After a few weeks, all students then write their information into five paragraphs with five underlined headings: Description, Food, Enemies, Habitat, and Interesting Facts. Each student creates a poster by gluing the report onto a large piece of colored paper and including a detailed drawing of the animal, which often takes more time and effort than the report itself. The reports are read aloud to the class, and then I have the pleasure of marking 5 paragraphs times 27 children on the amazing animals of the Arctic. Then, finally, I could return, guilt-free, to my classroom and dive back into the world of fiction!

I imagine that many of you reading this may be making several "connections" to my experience. And while it may sound as though I do not believe in the notion of nonfiction report writing, that is not the case. Research reports on animals are an essential part of students' learning; however, I now believe that there are important skills and strategies we need to teach students, *prior to* their independent study, that will enable them to have a more meaningful and thoughtful learning experience. Learning about text features, about asking questions, about making connections to background knowledge, and where to find the main idea—these are all prerequisites for any independent research.

1 What Is Nonfiction Reading Power?

Reading Power is an approach to teaching comprehension that focuses students' attention on their thinking and enables them to find meaning from texts based on their own ideas, experiences, and background knowledge. It is recognized as a practical approach to teaching a complex subject—how to teach students, not only to read thoughtfully, but also to articulate their thoughts using the appropriate language.

Reading comprehension and metacognition have become a much needed focus in many classrooms, schools, and school districts: district initiatives are being developed around it; professional books are being written about it; curriculums are being based on it; publishing companies are producing resources grounded in its principles. Teachers are recognizing that reading is not a subject that is taught only in the primary grades, but a subject that needs to continue to be taught throughout elementary school and beyond. They recognize that comprehension is often not a natural result of learning how to decode, and many are spending explicit instructional time teaching students *how to think* rather than *what to think*. Because of this new insight on the part of their teachers, many students are becoming aware that reading is more than just words on a page, but involves the reader interacting with, and weaving their thinking through the fabric of, the text. Nonfiction Reading Power

- is based on research that looks at strategies used by proficient readers.
- teaches students that reading is thinking.
- teaches students to be metacognitive, or aware of their thinking.
- creates a common "language of thinking" in your classroom and school.
- teaches students five powers to enhance their understanding of the information texts they are reading: the powers to Zoom-In, Determine Importance, Connect, Question/Infer, and Transform.
- encourages students to have "busy brains" while they read information.
- provides a concrete visual tool to help teach the five reading powers.
- can be used to enhance your writing program.
- integrates reading instruction with content learning.
- promotes content learning in an environment of thinking.
- will change the way you and your students read and think.

The Nonfiction Reading Power Strategies

The strategies you choose—whether they be from the list of strategies that make up the Strategies Used by a Proficient Reader (page 10), from the reading powers, or from another source—and the number you choose to introduce during the course of a year are not important. What is important is that everyone on your staff makes a commitment to intentionally integrate the strategies and the "language of thinking" into their daily practice. Creating a common language across the grades in a school becomes instrumental in a child's development as a reader.

There are five strategies that we will focus on to help students comprehend nonfiction or informational texts:

- **Zoom-In:** Active readers recognize, locate, and are able to interpret nonfiction text features.
- **Question/Infer:** Active readers ask questions and make inferences to further their understanding of nonfiction texts.
- **Determine Importance:** Active readers are able to find the main ideas in nonfiction texts
- **Connect:** Active readers make connections to experiences and background knowledge to enhance their understanding of nonfiction texts.
- **Transform (or Synthesize):** Active readers are able to recognize a change in their own thinking, perception, or perspective through reading a piece of nonfiction text.

With nonfiction, the order in which you teach the strategies is important. Nonfiction texts require the reader to use text features to find the information they need for the specific purpose; therefore, it is important for students to be introduced to this strategy first. Nonfiction texts are also based on inquiry, and the learning and extending of knowledge; therefore, readers need to sct the stage for this by asking the questions that will guide and focus their reading. Determining importance is the next strategy taught, as it is essential that students determine what the text is about before moving forward in their interactive and interpretive response to text. Connecting to personal experiences and background knowledge helps readers to extend their understanding by finding meaning. Transforming is introduced as the final merging of text and thinking.

The Reader as Thinker

Moving Into Thinking (page 16) is a visual representation of the strategies from a literal to an interactive reading experience. Any linear chart has its flaws and this one is no exception; thinking is never linear, but flows back and forth between levels. This chart does represent, however, thc difference between text and reader as thinker. The white space is the text being read; the shaded area represents the reader as thinker. Based on this, in the literal phase—a phase teachers tend to spend a large amount of instructional time focusing on—the text dominates over thinking. That is not to say that summarizing or finding the main ideas do not require thinking, but the emphasis in this phase of interpreting is on the text itself. Summarizing, determining importance, retelling, and story mapping are literal interpretations of the text. They are skills essential for readers to understand the content; however, for many teachers they represent the ultimate purpose of the reading lesson. Once the main idea has been determined, they move on to the next chapter. As important as they are, the acts of finding the main idea and summarizing are for me the beginning of interpreting text, not the end.

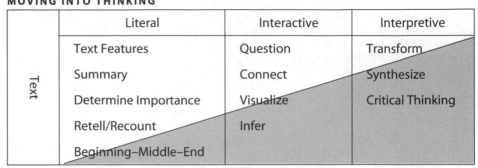

	Literal	Interactive	Interpretive
Text	Text Features	Question	Transform
	Summary	Connect	Synthesize
	Determine Importance	Visualize	Critical Thinking
	Retell/Recount	Infer	
	Beginning–Middle–End		

Reader As Thinker

This visual shows us where we need to go next with our students: we need to extend their thinking into the text. As it indicates, in the interactive stage of reading, a reader's thinking is as important as the text itself. The middle section is where we begin to teach students how to add their own thinking to the text to help enhance meaning. In the last level of understanding, the book itself almost doesn't matter anymore. What matters most is the reader's thinking and re-thinking of the text. Once the reader moves into the last level of understanding, it is clear that the text itself is no longer as important as the reader's thoughts.

I recall my own reading instruction being primarily in the first column of the Moving Into Thinking chart. As a student, I learned well how to summarize texts, having been given ample opportunities to master the strategy. I remember having marks taken off if I added my own thoughts into a summary I was assigned. I don't remember ever being taught how to infer; however, in high school I was expected to know how. I developed the Moving Into Thinking visual as a reminder to me where I want to be taking my students. I am no longer satisfied when they are able to summarize or tell me the main idea from a piece. I then want them to take that information and move toward a deeper understanding by adding their own thinking to the text. The lesson doesn't end when they have figured out what's in the text; the lesson ends when they have figured out what they think about it.

The Reading/Listening/Thinking Continuum

In 2006, our province released a new Language Arts Curriculum. The curriculum is centred on the *process* of literacy, rather than purpose or product. It has a strong emphasis on oral language as the foundation and springboard for both reading and writing. Part of my job as a literacy mentor in my district was to help teachers understand how the curriculum was organized. During my in-depth study of the 876-page document, I experienced a significant "ah-ha!" moment. I was looking at the learning outcomes for Oral Language, and thought I was on the wrong page—the learning outcomes were the same as those listed in the Reading and Viewing section: asking questions, retelling, making connections, visualizing, synthesizing, etc. I thought that there must have been some error and that the reading strategies were inserted in the wrong place. But after pondering this, I had a small epiphany. And since we are all familiar with the notion that Oral Language involves both speaking and listening, I started looking at Oral Language in terms of Productive (speaking, communicating ideas, sharing information) and Receptive (listening, processing information, understanding) skills.

"Lay down a foundation of thinking and then have them [the students] merge the content with their thinking."—David Perkins (1993)

ORAL LANGUAGE SKILLS

Productive	Receptive
• speaking	• listening
• communicating ideas	• processing information
• sharing information	• understanding

When someone is receiving language from another, it is not simply a matter of hearing what the person is saying. Listening is a metacognitive process, similar to reading, in which one is processing information. Whether I'm receiving the information visually from text or orally from someone speaking to me, I'm still processing the information in the same way. For example, when I listen to someone speak, I take in the information and sift it around in my thinking: I might be making a connection to what the person is saying; I might be wondering about something they are saying; I might be making an inference; or something that person just said might be enabling me to transform my thinking or synthesize my ideas more clearly. Lo and behold, the strategies I have been considering reading strategies are, in fact, the same strategies I use when I'm listening.

The conclusion derived from this "transformed thought" is that the reading strategies (or listening strategies, for that matter) are really *thinking* strategies. We think when we read, we think when we listen, we think when we write….

Many of us have spent time brainstorming with our students: "What does a good listener look like?" This might include such things as eye contact, "knee to knee," head nodding. But even after practicing and role playing good listening, there are students who look at their partners and nod their heads—but are thinking about recess.

A two-sided anchor chart for good listening can help students begin to see the metacognitive link between reading and listening.

GOOD LISTENERS…

On the outside:	On the inside:
• Make eye contact	• Make connections
• Face the speaker	• Ask questions
• Use appropriate body language	• Visualize
• Nod their heads	• Make inferences
• Say something: e.g., "great idea," "interesting point"	• Sometimes get new thoughts or ideas
	• Summarize
	• Remember important details

In classroom practice, invite students to make this connection between reading and listening on their own. Use the Good Listeners… anchor chart, and refer to reading strategies you have already covered in class. I prompt the discussion like this:

When you read, you need to be thinking about what you are reading. In the same way, a good listener needs to be thinking about what his or her partner is saying. I will be listening to you tell me something, and inside my head I might be visualizing what you are saying, or wondering something, or making a connection. Does anybody notice anything familiar about this side of the chart?

(Point to the strategies listed on the right side of the anchor chart)

Why would Reading Power strategies be listed on this Listening chart? Maybe they are not actually reading powers, but thinking powers! I think when I read, but I also think when I'm listening. The only difference is where the information is coming from. When I read, I'm using my eyes and getting the information from the book. When I listen, I'm using my ears and getting the information from the speaker. But my brain is actually doing the same thing – *thinking!*

As with all suggestions for lessons and reproducibles that appear in this book, you will likely want to modify this script to make it a perfect fit for your class and individual students. What is important is that your students experience the same "a-ha!" realization that I did: our brains use the same comprehension strategies when reading and when thinking.

Once the connection has been made between reading, listening, and thinking, the strategies students come to use when reading become applicable over a wide range of learning. Janice Novakowski, an experienced science consultant, has been exploring the many ways the strategies of questioning, visualizing, connecting, inferring, and synthesizing can be applied to many aspects of science. Carol Saundry, math consultant and respected workshop presenter, has long been promoting linking these thinking strategies with numeracy.

Using Nonfiction Reading Power

There are three important components of Reading Power:

1. The **Reading Power Model** represents the metacognitive piece of Reading Power, the importance of providing your students with the "big picture" of what reading and thinking are.
2. The **Nonfiction Booklists** are a way to organize the texts you will use; they reinforce the importance of selecting appropriate books to use in modeling, teaching, and practicing the strategies.
3. Most important is the **Method of Instruction**: how to actually teach these strategies in your classroom.

Chapters 3 to 7 will take you deeper into each of the Nonfiction Reading Power strategies. Each of these gives some insight into the strategy and suggestions on how to introduce the concept to your students. A series of teacher-directed and independent lessons take you through the steps of modeling, guiding, and independent practice. You will find student samples and reproducible charts and templates for use in your classroom.

Introducing Nonfiction

The first time I read the quote to the left, I was astounded. After my initial shock, I began to have some doubts about how accurate it was. And while the first part of the quote described my classroom, I begged to differ with the accuracy of the second part. I don't read nonfiction books by choice, and all the books that line the bookshelf in my living room are novels. So convinced was I that Stephanie Harvey (for whom I have the utmost respect) was wrong that I felt it was my duty to write to her and tell her that I was an exception.

I am thankful that letter was never written, because I have learned that my misconception of what "nonfiction" actually is had led me astray. One of the biggest misconceptions I have carried with me since childhood is that fiction and nonfiction were virtually the same – the only difference being that fiction was not true and nonfiction was true. But I realize now that nonfiction is not simply a book describing something, nor is it "equal" to fiction. If fiction is "the story," then nonfiction can be defined as "not a story"; i.e., virtually anything we read that is not a story.

Tony Stead describes an experiment he did to try to determine whether he read more fiction or nonfiction in a one-day period. I tried the same experiment, recording every eye-to-text experience in a 24-hour stretch: everything from the ingredients on a cereal box to a newsletter to instructions for a new board game. The results were shocking—of the 46 eye-to-text experiences I had, 42 were categorized as nonfiction. Had I not been a teacher and a parent, the amount of fiction would have been even lower. Prior to this experience, I had always considered fiction and nonfiction to be different, yet of equal value in the reading world. The chart below clearly, which lists examples from both genres, demonstrates that fiction and non-fiction are not equal—at least in terms of frequency. Nonfiction makes up most of the text we read in our world.

READING IN A 24-HOUR PERIOD

Fiction	Nonfiction	
• Fictional narrative	• recipes	• biographies
• Fairy tales	• instruction manuals	• catalogues
• Folk tales	• maps	• order forms
	• menus	• applications
	• programs	• résumés
	• newsletters	• letters to the editor
	• signs	• prescription bottle labels and monographs
	• magazines	
	• newspapers	• lists
	• faxes	• narrative nonfiction
	• e-mails	• advertisements and pamphlets
	• ingredients on food packaging	• want ads

Stephanie Harvey was absolutely right—the majority of the reading we do outside of school is nonfiction. So why am I spending so much time teaching children to read and write stories? What has new learning done to my practice? Certainly, I spend more time teaching my students not only how to read and understand nonfiction, but also helping them recognize that the world of nonfiction is not just the books we see in the library, but everything we read that is not a story.

If someone asked me to estimate how much time I spent on nonfiction versus fiction in my classroom (read-alouds, classroom library, reading and writing experiences) I would have to admit to spending 80% on fiction and 20% on nonfiction. I was determined to tip that scale to find a better balance, and committed to adding more nonfiction reading and writing into my literacy program. Rather than becoming overwhelmed with reconstructing my whole literacy program, I decided on three manageable things I could do to start adding more nonfiction into my classroom practice:

- nonfiction read-alouds
- a nonfiction author study
- teaching nonfiction forms and text structures.

Nonfiction Read-Alouds

Many children, particularly boys I've noticed, love to "get the facts." They love learning trivial tidbits of information that make up the world around us. *The Guinness Book of World Records* is the most frequently read book by boys both in my classroom and in my home. Reading aloud from fact books engages certain students in a way that reading fiction aloud rarely does. These books are great for quick read-alouds because they don't have to be read from cover to cover—any page will do! Just open it up and start reading.

Question and answer books can be a great hit in the classroom. Try reading the question out at the end of the day and then have the children think about it at home, maybe even asking their parents. The next morning, have the children discuss their thinking with a buddy, then read aloud the answer from the book. Later, have students take turns choosing the question from the book to share with the class.

> I love the fact that, in our profession, we get an opportunity to start fresh every year. I always take this fresh start as a new opportunity to reflect on my practice and see what I might be able to do differently or better.

> In all book lists:
> P = primary
> I = intermediate

BOOKS FOR GREAT NONFICTION READ-ALOUDS

Judy Allen, *Are You a Spider?* (The Backyard books also available: *Grasshopper, Ant, Bee, Dragonfly, Snail*) (P)

Dianna Aston, *An Egg is Quiet; A Seed is Sleepy* (P,I)

Melvin & Glida Berger, *Hurricanes Have Eyes But Can't See* (I)

Adele Ciboul, *The Five Senses* (P)

Anthony D. Fredericks, *In One Tidepool: Crabs, Snails and Salty Tails; Near One Cattail: Turtles, Logs and Leaping Frogs; In One Flower: Butterflies, Ticks and a Few More Icks* (P)

Vivian French, *Growing Frogs* (P)

Isabella Hatkoff, *Owen and Mzee* (companion book to Jeannette Winter, *Mama?*) (I)

Ben Hillman, *How Big Is It?; How Strong Is It?* (I)

Meredith Hooper & Lucia duLeiris, *The Island That Moved: How Shifting Forces Shape Our Earth* (I)

Grace Lin & Ranida McKneally, *Our Seasons* (P)

Wayne Lynch, *The Scoop on Poop* (I)

Meghan McCarthy, *Astronaut Handbook* (P)

Faith McNulty, *If You Decide to Go to the Moon; How To Dig A Hole to the Other Side of the Earth* (P)

Heather Lynn Miller, *This Is Your Life Cycle* (I)

Karen Orloff, *I Wanna Iguana* (P,I)

Steve Parker, *My Story of Life in a Pond* (P)

Sarah Peralta, *All About My Brother* (I)

Brigitte Raab, *Where Does Pepper Come From? And Other Fun Facts* (P)

Catherine Ripley, *WHY? The best ever question and answer book about science, nature and the world around you* (P,I)

James Solhein, *It's Disgusting and We Ate It!; Food Facts from Around the World* (I)
Tony Stead, *Should There Be Zoos?* (I)
I Wonder Why books (Kingfisher) (I)

Nonfiction Author Study

If you asked me to name a children's author of fiction, I could rattle off 25 names without blinking. But as recently as five years ago, the world of nonfiction authors for children was virtually unknown to me, with the exception of Gail Gibbons. So I set out to become acquainted with some new nonfiction authors. This was, indeed, a valuable experience, as I discovered many amazing authors and their extraordinary body of work.

My next step in integrating more nonfiction into my classroom was including a nonfiction author to my author study. I have always done an author study with my class every spring, focusing on the life and work of a particular author. Jez Alborough, Kevin Henkes, and Chris Van Allsburg are among the authors we studied. Because I was not familiar with any nonfiction authors, I had never focused on one. It was not difficult to adapt my framework for studying an author of nonfiction, and my class spent the next month exploring the life and work of Nicola Davies (see author study worksheet on page 22). The students were fascinated to learn about the life of this interesting woman. Learning that Nicola Davies is a marine biologist and that she studies firsthand the creatures she writes about was an important lesson for students in the validity, accuracy, and source of information in nonfiction texts.

Find out if authors have websites before including them on your list, as some are easier to get information on than others.

Using the gradual release of responsibility model, we focused on one author as a whole class, working through these sections together. Then the students chose their own nonfiction author to explore. I usually give them a list of five or six authors to choose from. Here is a list of nonfiction authors who have written a multitude of nonfiction books for children that I have found to work well for author studies.

Judy Allen	Kathryn Lansky
Michael Dahl	Claire Llewellyn
Nicola Davies	Peter Sis
Anthony D. Fredericks	Diane Swanson
Gail Gibbons	Seymour Simon
Deborah Hodge	Jan Thornhill
Steve Jenkins	Maxine Trottier
Stephan Kramer	Jeanette Winter

Nonfiction Forms and Structures

This breakdown of nonfiction texts into different forms, adapted from the work of Tony Stead, helps me and my students sort out and simplify the complex and vast world of nonfiction:

"The category of nonfiction is very broad and needs to be broken down to help children find what they need for their specific purpose"—Tony Stead (2002)

- Descriptive: organized facts about something (animal, insect, country, etc.)
- Instructional/procedural: sequential steps for making or doing something
- Explanatory: how or why something occurs, is made or works
- Persuasive: a supported opinion about a specific topic
- Biography: a linear recount and/or highlights the events of a person's life

Let's Explore a Nonfiction Author!

Name: _____   Date: _____

Name of author : _____

Place of birth: _____   Date of birth: _____

_____ 's family tree   My family tree

Childhood interests, experiences that may have influenced the author to become a writer:

Background, education, interests, hobbies:

Did you know…? Fascinating facts about _____

Questions I would like to ask _____ if I ever met him/her:

Titles by this author (please include publication date):

What things do you notice about the way this author writes? Style? Subject? Visuals?

What do you like most about this author?

A closer look at one of _____ 's books. Choose one book that the author has written and "tell a friend" about it. Include title, topic, brief summary, why you chose it, a connection you made, a question you have, an image that stuck in your mind after you closed the book (draw what you visualized), and tell something new that you learned from reading the book.

Lesson: Introducing Nonfiction Forms and Structures

For this lesson you will need
• a plastic tub with a lid, labeled *FICTION = THE STORY*
• in this tub, one picture book, one beginning chapter book, and one novel
• a plastic tub with a lid, labeled *NONFICTION = NOT A STORY*
• in this tub, a variety of nonfiction texts from all categories

This lesson is to help students develop an understanding of the breakdown of nonfiction, and introduce the idea of text structures.

• Begin the lesson:

I brought two tubs into the class this morning . As you can see, one is labeled *Fiction*, the other one says *Nonfiction*. Let's start looking at what's inside the Fiction tub. Before I open the tub, what would you expect to find inside this tub?

(Answers will vary: "books," "stories," etc.)

(Open the fiction tub and hold up the three books.)

Here is a picture book, a chapter book, and a novel. Now, what do we know about these books? I know that these are all different stories, but they all have something in common —something that is the same in all of them. What is the same is the way these stories are written—and we call the way any text is written its "text structure." A text structure is like the "skeleton" of a piece of writing. Even though these three books tell different stories, their text structure is the same: the "skeleton" of these stories are the same. It's kind of like humans—we all have the same skeleton on the inside, but our hair, eyes, bodies, and faces are different. All stories have the same skeleton, but their outsides are different – different characters, different settings, different problems.

• Remind students of the text structure of a story: setting, characters, plot; problem, solution; beginning, middle, end. Remind them that no matter what story you read, even though they sound like they are different stories, they all have the same text structure.
• Bring out the second tub.

Now let's take a look inside the Nonfiction tub. I used to think that nonfiction books were all the same – information. But, in fact, there are different kinds of nonfiction texts and each one has their own text structure. This tub seems to have a lot more in it than the fiction tub…. I wonder why that is?

(Take out the Description books and show them to students.)

Here are some nonfiction books—one about ladybugs, one about Africa, one about Mars, and another about different kinds of birds. All these books are different but, just like the fiction books, they all have something similar – a similar text structure or skeleton. Does anyone know what all these particular nonfiction texts have that is the same?

These nonfiction books are called *Descriptive* books because they all describe or tell about something—this one is describing an insect, this one a country—all different topics but all the same nonfiction structure.

• Continue to introduce the other forms of nonfiction in the same manner, with each new pile of books having a similar text structure. Each time you show a new group of books say:

These are all different but they all have a similar text structure. Let's think about how all these books are organized in a similar way.

Instructional: These texts all give instructions on how to do or make something:

Explanatory Texts: These texts all explain how something happens, most often a scientific phenomenon like how rainbows are formed, why leaves change color, or why snakes shed their skins.

Persuasive Texts: These texts all try to persuade me to do something, buy something, go somewhere. All of them tell us what they want us to do and then try to convince us to do that. They might try to convince us with words or with pictures.

Biography: These texts all retell the events of a real person. The events might include date of birth, place of birth, family, childhood, schooling, and what significant contribution this person made to the world. No matter who the person is in the book, you will find similar information in all of them.

- Reflection: What did you learn today?

  - A "text structure" is how a piece of writing is organized.
  - Fiction books have one main text structure: beginning, middle, end.
  - There are several different forms of nonfiction: descriptive, instructional, explanatory, persuasive, biography.
  - Each nonfiction form has its own text structure.
  - Being able to identify text structures can help us with our understanding of nonfiction books.

- Extension: Students can go home with a list of nonfiction forms and "collect" examples from each category. Or, mix up the nonfiction texts from the tub and have the students "sort" them into their correct categories.

Shelley Ledingham, Grade 7 teacher at Myrtle Beach Elementary, has her students identify the different nonfiction text structures while reading through newspapers and magazines.

2 The Components of Nonfiction Reading Power

The Model for Nonfiction Reading Powers

Years ago, I had a student in my class I would define as a "master decoder." He read fluently page after page, but had no idea what he was reading. One day, after he was unable to tell me anything about the two pages he had just read, I asked him, "Aren't you thinking about the story when you read it?" After a short pause, he responded with another question: "What does thinking look like?" At the time, I was unable to respond to his extraordinary question, but that experience and that question never left me.

This is the response of a Kindergarten student who was asked, "What does your brain look like when you're thinking?"

It is important that students have a metacognitive awareness of what happens when they read, and this led to the development of a model for the strategies or powers used in reading nonfiction. The Nonfiction Reading Powers model (page 29) helps to answer the question "What does thinking look like?" and provides students with a visual for thinking.

The Nonfiction Reading Powers model is an interactive, visual prompt for the during-reading process. Each model depicts a child's head and shoulders, with the phrase "Fill Your Brain with Nonfiction Reading Power!" at the top. There is a reproducible template of five separate, removable puzzle pieces that fit together and can be superimposed on the child's head. Each piece is labeled with a different nonfiction reading power, or strategy. As you introduce and teach each reading power, the appropriate puzzle piece is placed inside the image of the child's head. You can use the model as a way of providing students with a visual

Thinking, for many of us, is an abstract concept. It is not easily defined or easy to visualize.

and a framework for their thinking. By seeing what thinking looks like, students develop a metacognitive approach to reading, an awareness that reading is about thinking.

Because proficient readers often move from one reading power to another within a single reading experience, it is important to teach these reading powers accumulatively rather than separately. New pieces are added as new reading powers are introduced, but the puzzle pieces are never removed once placed in the head. Students will see that the brain becomes filled as their metacognitive knowledge of the five reading powers for nonfiction develops, demonstrating that good readers have many different things going on in their heads while they read. Once each strategy or Reading Power has been taught in isolation, we practice reading, thinking, and interacting with all of the strategies.

Lesson: Introducing the Nonfiction Reading Powers

This important concept lesson introduces students to metacognition, an awareness that reading is thinking.

For this lesson you will need
• chart paper or a SMART board for modeling
• the Nonfiction Reading Powers model (page 29)

• Begin the lesson: On chart paper or SMART board, sketch a large figure holding a book, with head left blank; you will be adding in parts of the lesson.

What body parts do you need to use when you read? What is each body part doing when you're reading? What are their jobs? Please share your thinking with your elbow partner.

It can be fun to suggest to primary students that they use their "x-ray" glasses (cardboard or plastic dollar-store sunglasses) to look deeply into the brain to see if they can tell "what thinking looks like."

• Invite students to share their responses. As they share, add body parts and labels to the visual. If "the brain" is mentioned, acknowledge the response and explain you would like to leave that for last.

The brain is a very important part of reading, but we often forget about it because it's an inside body part and we can't see it being used the way we can our hands or our eyes. When you are reading, your brain probably has many jobs—maybe more than one hundred—but today I want to talk about the "thinking jobs."

• Make reference to the Nonfiction Reading Powers model or poster, and proceed to place the thinking pieces in the visual of the head. Briefly explain each of the five reading powers.

Each thinking job helps you to understand the text you are reading better. As a good reader, you will use all of these "thinking jobs" or "reading powers" to help you think about what you are reading, and to understand it better.

Today, we're going to talk about what thinking jobs your brain has when you are reading information, or nonfiction. Your brain thinks a little differently than when you are reading a story, because what you are reading is different. When an active reader is reading nonfiction or informational texts, one of the first jobs their brain needs to do is Zoom-In on the special text features in that book. Text features help you locate information and organize that information for you.

(Place the *Zoom-In* puzzle piece in the head of the Nonfiction Reading Powers model.)

Good readers also Question when they read information. Asking questions helps readers think more deeply about the information. When you read information books, you often begin with a question, such as "I wonder if starfish can float?" or "Why can some birds fly and some can't?" and then we read to try to find the answer. Sometimes we find the answer in the book, but sometimes we don't. When our questions aren't answered, it can lead us to make an inference. To Infer is to add your own ideas into the text. Often there are things that are left out of a piece of text. As a good reader, you become a book detective and fill in the text with your own thinking.

(Place the *Question/Infer* puzzle piece in the head of the model.)

Another important thinking job your brain has when reading information is to try to figure out what's important. Nonfiction texts give readers a lot of information. Some of it is important; some of it might be details that are interesting details, but not necessarily important. Good readers know where to Determine Importance, how to sort out the important parts from the details.

(Place the *Determine Importance* puzzle piece in the head of the model.)

A fourth thinking job an active reader does is making a connection. Many of you know to Connect is to be able to find something in your own experiences to help you understand the text better. When we connect to stories, we often make connections to personal experiences: "That reminds me of the time when I…" Connecting to nonfiction might look a little different. If I'm reading about Mars, for example, I may not be able to make a connection to a personal experience, because I've never been to Mars. I can, however, make a connection to something that I already know about Mars. This is called "connecting to background knowledge."

(Place the *Connect* puzzle piece in the head of the model.)

The last thinking job that a reader can do when reading information is to Transform. That does not mean that reading can turn us into robots—but it does mean that sometimes reading can change our thinking. We have an idea, then we read, and something in what we read mixes with that idea, and then the idea changes. To Transform is to experience a change in your thinking, a new thought or a new way of looking at something.

(Place the *Transform* puzzle piece in the head of the model.)

- Reflection: After this lesson, I like to invite students to reflect on what they learned about reading. See What I Learned About Reading Today template on page 30.
- The Nonfiction Reading Powers model (page 29) can be copied and distributed to students at the end of this lesson. Students can add identifying features and clothing to the figure, as well as the thinking pieces.

Nonfiction Reading Powers

Fill Your Brain with Nonfiction Reading Powers!

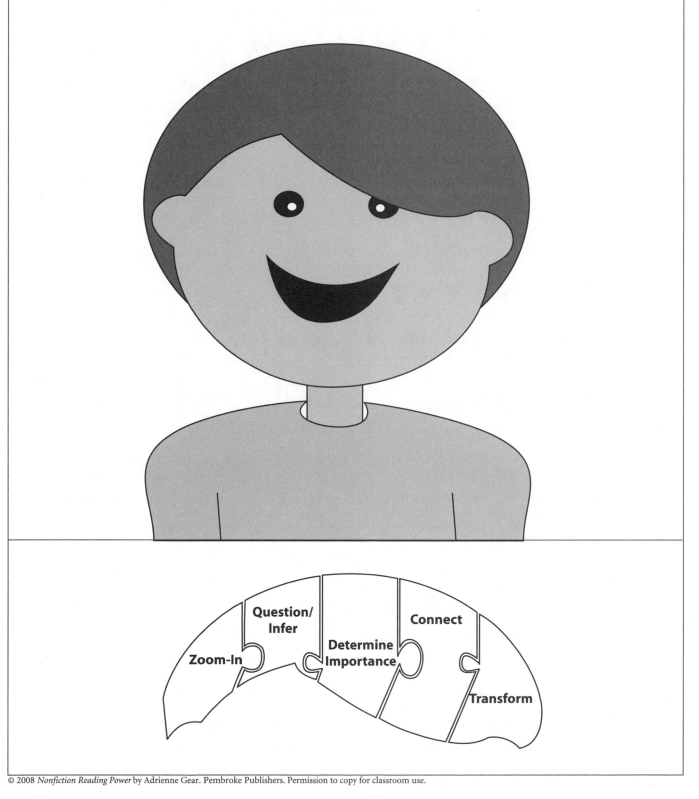

What I Learned About Reading Today

Name: _____

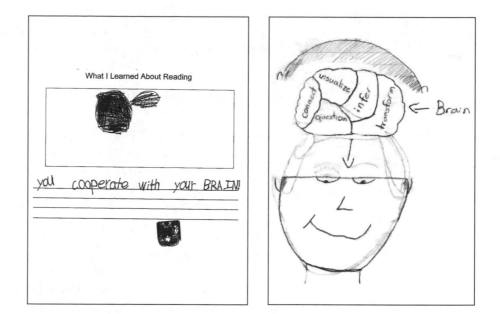

Our goal is to help our students develop the strategies to become independent thinkers, and isolating the strategies initially is important for their learning. However, if they are left with the concept that the Nonfiction Reading Powers exist in isolation, they will have a difficult time putting them together to become independent thinkers and effective readers of information.

A teacher called me into her room to show me her use of the Reading Powers model. "I've made the head a wig," she explained. She had permanently stuck the pieces of the brain inside the poster and covered the pieces with "a wig" that had "windows" that she could open, revealing the Reading Power(s) inside!

The Big Picture

Watching the Reading Powers model being used in classrooms, I've noticed that sometimes the only piece visible to the students is the strategy being taught. Teachers begin the year, the poster goes up, the first strategy is placed into the brain, and the modeling and practicing begins. There is no reference, however, to the big picture, the goal we are working toward: to have a full, thinking, interactive brain engaged in text. By not introducing all the strategies first, and not having all the pieces visible at all times, we may be promoting comprehension as isolated strategies rather than strategic thinking.

Unfortunately, I have overheard, on more than one occasion, that "the best part about Reading Power is, in June, when all the pieces are in the brain on my poster and I've taught all the strategies—I'm finished!" Once all the strategies have been taught, yes, there is cause for celebration; however, you are not finished, but rather just beginning. The real power of Reading Power comes *after* the strategies have been taught, when the students begin to apply the strategies to any book. It is crucial that we, as teachers, recognize the difference between teaching our students a list of strategies and teaching our students to become strategic readers and thinkers.

I do believe it to be absolutely essential that, when students are first being introduced to these strategies, and when they are just beginning to develop their awareness of thinking and the language to articulate it, these strategies must be taught separately. The poster with the brain pieces contributes to this concept, as you "add" into the brain as you teach. However, if we don't help students move beyond the isolation of the strategies, we risk missing the most important part of the process: application.

The Reading Powers model has been adapted by many different teachers for their classrooms. Some have created their own visual to display, or have had students create their own. Others have provided a master for children to make their own visual that can be added to as each new Reading Power is introduced. Edward (Woody) Bradford, principal in Abbotsford, finds he does not need the actual poster to demonstrate metacognition; instead, he sticks the brain pieces onto his own forehead when he visits classrooms and models reading and thinking! (This unique idea has been quite a hit with his students; however, I understand it can produce what is now known as a "reading rash"!)

Nonfiction Book Collections

Nonfiction texts are structured differently than narrative fiction. We often don't read a nonfiction book cover to cover in one sitting, as we would with a picture book. Nonfiction texts are structured in a way that the reader can read smaller sections of text; therefore when teaching these strategies with informational texts, we are using small chunks of text, or short articles or chapters, rather than the whole book.

In this book, the lessons can be taught with any number of different texts. When booklists are followed too closely and relied on too heavily, it can result in a lack of conceptual understanding of the strategy. While specific books will be recommended for each strategy, my goal is for teachers to understand the strategy well enough that they will learn to leave the harbor and sail independently with their own books and other nonfiction resources.

I believe that looking at reading strategies from the perspective of nonfiction reading is an opportunity to integrate content areas into your teaching. Using books that are connected to units you are covering in class when modeling and practicing the reading powers promotes focused learning. Let's face it—it is difficult to fit everything in, so it makes sense to try to cover your content while teaching the strategies. By providing a generic, as opposed to content-centred, approach, I hope you are more likely to use the strategy lessons with books specific to your content area.

It is important to note that the recommended nonfiction resources in this chapter are trade books that can be purchased through book stores. Don't think, however, that the lessons will work only if you purchase all the books. The lessons have been designed in such a way that you can use a variety of texts, including your classroom textbooks, guided reading sets, newspapers, and magazine articles. Also, be mindful of the media and technology texts that students encounter on a daily basis. The strategies presented in the lesson outlines can also be applied to information found and read online.

Suggested Topics

Readers will learn to **Zoom-In** when reading texts that

- utilize many nonfiction text features; e.g., maps, charts, diagrams, webs, comparisons, captions, visuals, italics, bold headings

Readers will learn to **Question/Infer** when reading texts that

- promote "deep thinking"
- are designed around questions
- are content-based, with topics that they may be exploring in class
- include wordless images or photographs
- don't include all the information, or are open-ended in nature

Readers will learn to **Determine Importance** when reading texts that

- are short: 1–2-page articles, chapters, or pieces that are more text heavy

---

With fiction, books are organized around the strategies. While strategy or reading power remains a consideration with nonfiction book organization, content and subject area become more important considerations. In this book, booklists are organized with both strategy and subject area in mind.

District science consultant Janice Novakowski finds that it just makes more sense to do Nonfiction Reading Power work with the science or social studies content you are teaching. She recommends teachers create Topic Tubs for use in classrooms as a way of covering content and strategies simultaneously. The books in each tub are labeled with the strategy or strategies that most directly apply.

- include text features
- represent a variety of text structures (description, instruction, persuasion, etc.)

Readers will learn to **Connect** to text when reading books that

- are based in content with which students have both personal experience and background knowledge; e.g., animals, plants, weather, community, family, children around the world
- are content-based, with topics that they may be exploring in class

Readers will learn to **Transform** their thinking when reading texts that

- include quick facts that stimulate big reactions
- introduce readers to thought-provoking issues in the world: e.g., global warming, animal extinction, earth's water supply, amazing creatures or natural wonders
- describe the lives of extraordinary and/or inspiring people who have made an impact on the world

Reading Power is not grounded in any book or tub of books. It is grounded in the principles of thinking and metacognition. Using books to model, teach, and practice the strategies is a means of helping students develop as thinkers, but not necessarily a means to an end. The "end" is when your students are able to use any Reading Power with any book.

Booklists by Subject

RA—Read-Aloud
Z—Zoom-In
Q/I—Question/Infer
DI—Determining Importance
C—Connect
T—Transform

These booklists are organized around specific science and social studies topics, to provide teachers with a starting point for modeling and guided practice. Because the strategy lessons are designed generically, teachers can choose a book to use for the lesson that fits into their content area.

The books have been cross-referenced to lessons for specific strategies. The grades listed are suggested levels only. Certainly, within a class, students will exhibit a diverse range of abilities. Teachers may choose to create topic collections that cover a range of reading levels.

Life Science: Animal Growth and Change

EARLY PRIMARY/K–1

Margaret Carney, *Where Does a Tiger-Heron Spend the Night?*

Michael Dahl, *Do Frogs Have Fur? A Book About Animal Coats and Coverings* (Other titles include: *Do Cows Eat Cake: A Book About What Animals Eat; Do Ducks Live in the Dessert: A Book About Where Animals Live; Do Goldfish Gallop: A Book About Animal Movement; Do Whales Have Wings: A Book About Animal Bodies*)

DK Publishing, *Mammal* (Series: Eye Know)

Deborah Heiligman, *From Caterpillar to Butterfly*

Pamela Hickman, *A New Frog: A First Look at the Lifecycle of an Amphibian* (ZI) (Series: A First Look at Nature; other titles include *Ducks; Butterflies*)

John Himmelman, *A House Spider's Life* (Series: Nature Upclose; other titles include: *A Monarch Butterflies Life; A Salamander's Life; A Ladybug's Life*)

Sam Godwin, *The Trouble with Tadpoles*

Claire Llewellyn, *Is That A Butterfly?: A Lift the Flap Life Cycle Story*

Claire Llewellyn, *How Animals Grow* (Series: I Know That!)

Wendy Pfeffer, *From Tadpole to Frog* (Series: Let's Read and Find Out About Science)

Editors of TIME for Kids, *TIME for Kids: Bees*

Laura Vaccaro Seeger, *First The* (T)

LATE PRIMARY/GRADE 2–3

Judy Allen, *Are You A Bee?* (Series: Backyard Books; other titles include: *Are you A Grasshopper?; Are You a Snail?; Are You a Butterfly?; Are You a Spider?*) (RA)

Diana Hutts Aston, *An Egg is Quiet* (RA)

Jacob Berowitz, *Jurassic Poop*

DK Publishing, Panda (Series: Watch Me Grow; other titles include: *Bear; Frog; Penguin; Butterfly*)

Vivian French, *Growing Frogs* (RA)

Deborah Hodge, *Ants* (Q/I)

Deborah Hodge, *Bees* (Q/I)

Steve Jenkins, *Actual Size* (RA)

Steve Jenkins, *Biggest, Fastest, Strongest* (T)

Bobbie Kalman, *The ABC's of Animals*

Bobbie Kalman, *What is a Life Cycle?*

Etta Kaner, *Animal Defences: How Animals Protect Themselves*

Claire Llewellyn, *Earthworms* (Series: Minibeasts; other titles include: *Spiders; Ladybugs; Caterpillars*)

Steve Parker, *It's a Frog's Life: My Story of Life in a Pond* (RA)

Angela Royston, *Looking at Life Cycles: How Do Plants and Animals Change?* (Series: Looking at Science: How Things Change)

Suzanne Slade, *What Do You Know About Life Cycles?* (Series: 20 Questions: Science)

Belinda Weber, *I Wonder Why Caterpillars Eat So Much and Other Questions about Life Cycles* (Series: I Wonder Why)

Nicola Davies, *Extreme Animals* (DI)

Nicola Davies, *Poop* (DI)

Cheryl Jakab, *The Animal Life Cycle 7* (Series: Earth's Cycles)

Bobbie Kalman, *The Life Cycle of a Spider* (Series: The Life Cycle; other titles include: *Life Cycle of a Frog; Life Cycle of a Bird; Life Cycle of a Butterfly*)

Heather Lynn Miller, *This is Your Life Cycle* (RA)

Seymour Simon, *Animals Nobody Loves* (ZI)

Diane Swanson, *Bugs Up Close* (DI)

Rochelle Strauss, *Tree of Life: The Incredible Biodiversity of Life on Earth*

Jan Thornhill, *I Found a Dead Bird: The kids guide to the cycle of life and death*

Life Science: Plant Growth and Change

Clyde Robert Bulla, *A Tree is a Plant* (Series: Let's Read and Find Out About Science)

Lois Ehlert, *Red Leaf, Yellow Leaf* (RA)

Allan Fowler, *From Seed to Plant* (Series: Rookie Read-About Science) (RA)

Carole Gerber, *Winter Trees* (RA)

Carole Gerber, *Leaf Jumpers* (RA)

Sam Godwin, *From Little Acorns: A First Look at the Life Cycle of a Tree*

Pamela Hickman, *A Seed Grows: My First Look at a Plant's Life Cycle* (Series: My First Look at Nature)

Helene Jordon, *How a Seed Grows* (Series: Let's Read and Find Out About Science)

Bobbie Kalman, *Plants are Living Things*

Gerald Legg, *From Seed to Sunflower* (Series: Lifecyles)

Claire Llewellyn, *Starting Life: Tree* (Series: Starting Life)

Helen Orme, *Why Do Plants Grow In Spring?*

Wendy Pfeffer, *From Seed to Pumpkin* (Series: Let's Read and Find Out About Science)

Anne Rockwell, *One Bean*

Angela Royston, *How Plants Grow* (Series: Heinemann First: Plants)

Editors of TIME for Kids, *TIME for Kids: Plants*

Ellen Weiss, *From Pit to Peach Tree* (Series: Scholastic News Nonfiction Readers: How Things Grow; other titles include: *From Pinecone to Pinetree; From Bulb to Daffodil; From Kernel to Corncob*)

Diana Hutts Aston, *A Seed Is Sleepy* (RA)

Andrew Charman, *I Wonder Why Trees Have Leaves and Other Questions About Plants* (Series: I Wonder Why)

Joanna Cole, *Magic School Bus Plants Seeds*

Gail Gibbons, *From Seed to Plant*

Victoria Huseby, *Oak Tree* (Series: Looking At Life Cycles)

Ontario Science Centre, *Plants*

Michael Ross, *Life Cycles*

Laurie Purdie Salas, *From Seed To Maple Tree: Following the Life Cycle*

Louise & Richard Spilsbury, *Why Do Plants Have Flowers?* (Series: World of Plants; other titles include: *What is a Plant?; How Do Plants Grow?*) (ZI)

Linda Tagliaferro, *The Life Cycle of an Oak Tree* (Series: Pebble Plus; other titles include *The Life Cycle of a Pine Tree; The Life Cycle of an Apple Tree; The Life Cycle of a Sunflower*)

Molly Aloian & Bobbie Kalman, *The Life Cycle of a Flower*

Jonathan Bocknek, *Plants* (Series: Life Science)

Honor Head, *Amazing Plants* (Series: Amazing Life Cycles)

Clare Hibbert, *The Life of a Tree* (Series: Life Cycles Up Close)

Pamela Hickman, *The Canadian Tree Book*

Cheryl Jakab, *The Plant Life Cycle* (Series: Earth's Cycles)

Bobbie Kalman, *What is a Plant?* (Series: The Science of Living Things)

Bobbie Kalman, *The Life Cycle of a Tree*

Claire Llewellyn, *Exploring Plants* (Series: A Sense of Science)

Claire Llewellyn, *The Life of Plants* (Series: Understanding Plants)

Valerie Wyatt, *Wacky Plant Cycles*

Life Science: Ecosystems/Food Chains/Habitats

EARLY PRIMARY/K–1

Susan Canizares, *Arctic Winter, Arctic Summer* (Series: Science Emergent Readers)

Madeleine Dunphy, *Here is the Wetland* (Other titles include: *Here is the African Savanna; Here is the Arctic Winter; Here is the Coral Reef; Here is the Tropical Rainforest*)

Anthony D. Fredericks, *In One Tidepool: Crabs, Snails, and Salty Tails* (Series: Sharing Nature With Children; other titles include: *Under One Rock: Bugs, Slugs, and Other Ughs; Near One Cattail: Turtles, Logs And Leaping Frogs; Around One Cactus: Owls, Bats and Leaping Rats*)

Gallimard Jeunesse, *The Rainforest*

Pamela Hickman, *Habitats*

Pamela Hickman, *Hungry Animals: A First Look at Food Chains*

Bobbie Kalman, *Homes of Living Things* (Series: Introducing Living Things)

Margriet Ruurs, *In My Backyard*

Jennifer Ward, *Somewhere in the Ocean* (Other titles include: *Way Up in the Arctic; Way Out in the Desert; Over in the Garden*)

Brenda Williams, *Home for a Tiger, Home for a Bear*

LATE PRIMARY/GRADE 2–3

Deborah Hodge, *Who Lives Here? Desert Animals* (Series: Who Lives Here?; other titles include: *Rain Forest Animals; Polar Animals; Wetland Animals*)

Bobbie Kalman, *ABC's of Habitats*

Bobbie Kalman, *ABC's of Oceans*

Bobbie Kalman, *Food Chains and You*

Steve Jenkins, *What Do You Do When Something Wants to Eat You?* (T)

Patricia Lambar, *Who Eats What?* (Series: Let's Read and Learn About Science)

Vic Parker, *Homes* (Series: What Living Things Need)

Wendy Pfeffer, *A Log's Life*

Frank Serafini, *Looking Closely Across the Desert* (Other titles include: *Looking Closely Along the Shore; Looking Closely Inside the Garden; Looking Closely Through the Forest*)

Suzanne Slade, *What Do You Know About Food Chains and Food Webs?* (Series: 20 Questions: Science)

Louise & Richard Spilsbury, *Where Do Plants Grow?* (Series: World of Plants)

David Stewart, *Pond Life* (Series: Cycles of Life)

David Suzuki & Sarah Ellis, *Salmon Forest*

Angela Wilkes, *Animal Homes*

INTERMEDIATE/GRADE 4–7

Harriet Brown, *Deserts* (Series: World About Us— written as "text on two levels", allowing for students of mixed reading levels to enjoy the same book; other titles include: *Rainforests; Seashores*)

Cheryl Jakab, *The Food Cycle* (Series: Earth's Cycles)

Rebecca L. Johnson, *A Journey Into a Wetland* (Series: Biomes of North America; other titles include: *A Walk in the Tundra; A Journey Into a Lake*)

Bobbie Kalman, *Food Chains and You* (Series: Food Chains; other titles include: *Coral Reef Food Chains; Seashore Food Chains; Tundra Food Chains; Forest Food Chains*)

Dorothy Hinshaw Patent, *Garden of Spirit Bear: Life in the Great Northern Rainforest*

Donald M. Silver, *Seashore* (Series: One Small Square; other titles include: *Coral Reef; Pond; Backyard; Woods*)

Suzanne Slade, *What Do You Know About Food Chains?* (Series: 20 Questions: Science)

Darlene R. Stille, *Tropical Rainforest* (Series: True Books: Ecosystems; other titles include: *Oceans; Grasslands; Wetlands*)

Life Science: The Human Body

Aliki, *I'm Growing*

Aliki, *My Five Senses*

Bob Barner, *Dem Bones*

Wiley Belvins, *Where Does Your Food Go?* (Series: Rookie Read-About Health; other books include: *How Does Your Brain Work?; How do Your Lungs Work?; How Does Your Heart Work?*)

DK Publishing, *Body* (Series: Eye Know)

Gallimard Jeunesse, *The Human Body*

Sharon Gordon, *Hearing* (Series: Rookie Read-About Health; other titles include: *Seeing; Feeling; Smelling*)

Bobbie Kalman, *I Am A Living Thing*

Maria Rius, *Taste* (Other books include: *Sight; Smell; Touch; Sound*)

Nuria Roca, *The Five Senses* (Series: Let's Learn About)

Kathy Stinson, *The Bare Naked Book*

Joan Sweeny, *Me and My Amazing Body*

Joan Sweeny, *Me and My Senses*

Stephanie Turnbull, *Your Body* (Series: Usborne Beginners; other titles include *Why Do We Eat?*)

LATE PRIMARY/GRADE 2–3

Brigid Avison, *I Wonder Why I Blink* (Series: I Wonder Why) (Q)

Philip Balestrino, *The Skeleton Inside You* (Series: Let's Read and Find Out About Science)

Melvin Berger, *Why I Sneeze, Shiver, Hiccup and Yawn* (Series: Let's Read and Find Out About Science)

Patty Carratello, *My Body*

Deborah Chancellor, *I Wonder Why Lemons Taste Sour and Other Questions About Senses* (Series: I Wonder Why)

Adele Ciboul, *The Five Senses*

Joanna Cole, *First Human Body Encyclopedia*

Joanna Cole, *You Can't Smell A Flower With Your Ear* (Series: All Aboard Science Reader)

Katharine Kenah, *The Bizarre Body* (series: Extreme Readers)

Michael Ross, *Body Cycles*

Paul Showers, *A Drop of Blood*

Paul Showers, *What Happens to a Hamburger?*

Herve Tullet, *The Five Senses*

Harriet Ziefert, *You Can't Taste a Pickle With Your Ear*

INTERMEDIATE/GRADE 4–7

Nick Arnold, *Blood, Bones and Body Bits*

Frances R. Balkwill, *Have a Nice DNA*

Melvin Berger, *Why Don't Haircuts Hurt?* (Series: Scholastic Q&A)

Sylvia Branzei, *Grossology and You*

DK Publishing, *Eyewitness Visual Dictionary of the Human Body*

John Farndon, *Human Body: The Ultimate Guide to How the Body Works* Jayne Parsons, *Encyclopedia of the Human Body*

Trudee Romanek, *Wow! The Most Interesting Book You'll Ever Read About the Five Senses* (Series: Mysterious You; other titles include: *Achoo! The Most Interesting Book You'll Ever Read About Germs; Ah-Ha! The Most Interesting Book You'll Ever Read About Intelligence*)

Barbara Seuling, *From Head to Toe: The Amazing Human Body and How it Works*

Seymour Simon, *The Heart* (Other titles include: *The Brain; Guts; Digestive System; Muscles; Bones; Eyes; Ears*)

Richard Walker, *The Kingfisher First Human Body Encyclopedia*

Earth Science: Planets and Solar System

EARLY PRIMARY/K–1

Frank Asch, *The Sun is My Favorite Star*

Byron Bauton, *I Want To Be An Astronaut*

DK Publishing, *Space* (Series: Eye Know)

Jennifer Dussling, *Stars* (Series: All Aboard Science Reader)

Edana Eckart, *Watching the Moon* (Series: Welcome Books: Watching Nature; other titles include: *Watching the Sun; Watching Stars; Watching the Sun*)

Allan Fowler, *So That's How the Moon Changes Shape* (Series: Rookie Read-About Science)

Tish Rabe, *There's No Place Like Space: All About Our Solar System* (Series: Cat in the Hat's Learning Library)

Scholastic, *The Universe*

Joan Sweeny, *Me and My Place in Space*

Editors of TIME for KIDS, *Planets! Discover Our Solar System*

Stephanie Turnbull, *Sun, Moon and Stars*

Lynn Wilson, *What's Out There? A Book About Space*

Franklyn M. Branley, *The Planets in Our Solar System* (Series: Let's Read and Find Out About Science; other titles include: *The Sky is Full of Stars; The Moon Seems to Change; Floating in Space*)

Janis Campbell, *G is for Galaxy: An Out of this World Alphabet*

DK Publishing, *Space* (Series: Eye Wonder)

Gail Gibbons, *The Planets*

Gail Gibbons, *Stargazers*

Mike Goldsmith, *Solar System* (Series: Kingfisher Young Knowledge)

Steve Jenkins, *Looking Down*

Katharine Kenah, *Space Mysteries* (Series: Extreme Readers)

Loreen Leedy, *Postcards from Pluto*

Meghan McCarthy, *Astronaut Handbook* (P)

Cynthia Pratt Nicolson, *Discover the Stars* (Series: Kids Can Read; other titles include: *Discover Space; Discover Space Rocks; Discover Planets*)

Leoni Pratt, *Planet Earth*

Usborne First Encyclopedia, *Space*

DK Publishing, *First Space Encyclopedia*

DK Publishing, *Space Facts* (Series: Pockets Guides; other titles include *Earth Facts*)

Joan Marie Galat, *Stories of Planets* (Series: Dot to Dot in the Sky; other titles include *Stories in the Stars; Stories of the Moon*)

Cynthia Pratt Nicolson, *Comets, Asteroids and Meteorites*

Cynthia Pratt Nicolson, *The Jumbo Book of Space*

Cynthia Pratt Nicolson, Space (Series: Starting With Space; other titles include: *The Earth; The Moon; The Planets; The Stars; The Sun*)

Elaine Scott, *When is a Planet Not a Planet? The Story of Pluto*

Seymour Simon, *Comets, Meteors and Asteroids*

Whitecap Books, *Space* (Series: Investigate)

Valerie Wyatt, *Space FAQ's*

Editors of YES magazine, *The Amazing International Space Station*

Earth Science: Weather

Frank Asch, *Like a Windy Day*

Susan Canizares, *Storms* (Series: Science Emergent Readers)

Vicki Cobb, *I Face the Wind*

Vicki Cobb, *I Get Wet*

DK Publishing, *Weather* (Series: Eye Know)

Edana Eckart, *Watching the Weather* (Series: Welcome Books: Watching Nature)

Allan Fowler, *Can You See the Wind?*

Allan Fowler, *What Do You See In A Cloud?* (Series: Rookie Read-About Science)

Tish Gabe, *Oh Say, Can You Say, What's the Weather Today?* (Series: Cat in the Hat Learning Library)

Gail Gibbons, *Weather Words and What they Mean*

Monica Hughes, *Weather Patterns* (Series: Nature's Patterns)

Etta Kaner, *Who Likes the Sun?* (Other books include: *Who Likes the Wind?; Who Likes the Snow?; Who Likes the Rain?*)

Katharine Kenah, *Wild Weather* (Series: Extreme Readers)

Faye Robinson, *Where Do Puddles Go?* (Series: Rookie Read-About Science)

Simon Adams, *The Best Book of Weather*

Franklyn M. Branley, *Down Comes the Rain*

Franklyn M. Branley, *Flash, Crash, Rumble and Roll*

Tomie de Paola, *The Cloud Book*

Lynda DeWitt, *What Will the Weather Be?* (Series: Let's Read and Find Out About Science)

Arthur Dorros, *Feel the Wind*

Helen Frost, *The Water Cycle*

B. A. Hoena, *Weather ABC: An Alphabet Book*

Bobbie Kalman, *The Water Cycle*

Marie-Anne Legault, *Scholastic Atlas of Weather*

Pat Michaels, *W is for Wind: A Weather Alphabet*

Marilyn Singer, *On the Same Day in March: A Tour of The World's Weather*

Neil Waldman, *Snowflake: A Water Cycle Story*

Melvin Berger, *Hurricanes Have Eyes But Can't See: And Other Amazing Facts About Wild Weather*

Melvin & Glida Berger, *Can It Rain Cats and Dogs?* (Series: Scholastic Q&A; other titles include: *Do Tornadoes Really Twist?*)

Julie Hannah, *The Man Who Named Clouds*

Bobbie Kalman, *Changing Weather: Storms*
Steven P. Kramer, *Lightning*
Steven P. Kramer, *Tornadoes*
Thomas Locker, *Cloud Dance*
Thomas Locker, *Water Dance*
Seymour Simon, *Weather*

Mark Shulman, *Super Storms that Rocked the World*
David Suzuki, *Looking At Weather*
John Woodward, *Weather Watcher* (Series: DK Nature Activities)
Valerie Wyatt, *Weather FAQ's*

Earth Science: Extreme Environments

EARLY PRIMARY/K-1

Katharine Kenah, *Extreme Planet* (Series: Extreme Readers)

LATE PRIMARY/GRADE 2-3

Sheldon Brooks, *Life in the Arctic*
Merideth Hooper, *Ice Trap! Shackleton's Incredible Expedition*
Claire Llewellyn, *Survive at Sea*
Anne Schreiber, *Volcanoes!* (Series: National Geographic KIDS)

INTERMEDIATE/GRADE 4-7

Nicola Davies, *Extreme Animals* (DI)
Broughton Coburn, *Triumph on Everest: A Photobiography of Sir Edmund Hillary*
Kathy Conlan, *Under the Ice*
Steve Jenkins, *Hottest, Coldest, Highest, Deepest*
Steve Jenkins, *On Top of the World* (T)
Laurie Skreslet, *To the Top of Everest*
Holly Wallace, *The Mysteries of Atlantis*
Christine Webster, *Glaciers*

Earth Science: Daily and Seasonal Change

EARLY PRIMARY/K-1

Robin Bernard, *A Tree for All Seasons*
Stella Blackstone, *Skip Through the Seasons*
Megan Montague Cash, *What Makes the Seasons?*
Edana Eckart, *Watching the Seasons* (Series: Welcome Books)
Allan Fowler, *How Do You Know it's Fall?* (Series: Rookie Read-About Science; other titles include: *How Do You Know it's Winter?*; *How Do You Know it's Spring?*; *How Do You Know it's Summer?*)
Carole Gerber, *Leaf Jumpers*
Linda Glasser, It's Spring (See also: *It's Fall; It's Winter; It's Summer*)
Ann Herriges, *Winter* (Series: Blast Off Readers! Seasons; other titles include *Spring; Summer; Fall*)
Claire Llewellyn, *Paint a Sun in the Sky: A First Look at Seasons*
Victoria Parker, *Days Out in Winter* (Series: Little Nippers; other books include: *Days Out in Spring; Days Out in Summer*)
Nuria Roca, *Summer* (Series: Four Seasons; other titles include *Fall; Spring; Winter*)
Anne Rockwell, *Four Seasons Make A Year*
June Young, *Look How It Changes* (Series: Rookie Read-About Science)

LATE PRIMARY/GRADE 2-3

Robin Bernard, *A Tree for All Seasons*
Franklyn M. Branley, *Sunshine Makes the Seasons*
Franklyn M. Branley, *What Makes Night and Day?*
Gail Gibbons, *The Reason for Seasons*
Gail Gibbons, *The Seasons of Arnold's Apple Tree*
Bobbie Kalman, *Changing Seasons*
Grace Lin & Ranida McKneally, *Our Seasons*
Claire Llewellyn, *Day and Night* (Series: I Know That: Cycles of Nature)
Betsy Maestro, *Why Do Leaves Change Color?*
Michael Ross, *Earth Cycles*
Angela Royston, *Looking At Weather and Seasons: How Do They Change?*
David Stewart, *Seasons* (Series: Cycles of Life)
Brenda Walpole, *I Wonder Why the Sun Rises and Other Questions About Time and Seasons* (Series: I Wonder Why...)

INTERMEDIATE/GRADE 4-7

Sylvia A. Johnson, *How Leaves Change*
Annie Jones, *The Four Seasons: Uncovering Nature*

Earth Science: Air, Water, Soil

EARLY PRIMARY/K–1

Frank Asch, *Water*

Susan Canizares, *Water* (Series: Science Emergent Readers)

Alan Fowler, *It Could Still Be Water* (Series: Rookie Read-About Science)

Sam Godwin, *The Drop Goes Plop: A First Look At the Water Cycle*

Gordon Morrison, *A Drop of Water*

Emily Neye, *Water* (Series: All Aboard Science Reader)

Michael Elsohn Ross, *Re-Cycles* (Series: Cycles)

LATE PRIMARY/GRADE 2–3

Christin Ditchfield, *Soil* (Series: True Books: Natural Resources)

Arthur Durros, *Follow The Water From Brook To Ocean* (Series: Let's Read and Find Out About Science)

Helen Frost, *Water as a Liquid* (See also: Water as A Solid; Water as A Gas)

Bobbie Kalman, *The Water Cycle*

Barbara Kerley, *A Cool Drink of Water*

Rebecca Olien, *The Water Cycle* (Series: First Facts: Water All Around)

Victoria Parker, *Air* (Series: What Living Things Need)

Victoria Parker, *Water* (Series: What Living Things Need)

Natalie M. Rosinsky, *Dirt: The Scoop on Soil*

Natalie M. Rosinsky, *Water Up and Down and All Around*

Alvin Silverstein, *Life in a Bucket of Soil*

Steve Tomecek, *Dirt* (Series: Jump Into Science)

Neil Waldman, *The Snowflake: A Water Cycle Story*

INTERMEDIATE/GRADE 4–7

Raymond Bial, *A Handful of Dirt*

Paulette Bourgeois, *The Dirt on Dirt*

Anita Ganeri, *Water Cycle* (Series: Nature's Patterns)

Beth Gurney, *Sand and Soil*

Cheryl Jakab, *The Water Cycle* (Series: Earth's Cycles)

David L. Lindbo, *SOIL! Get the Inside Scoop*

Barbara McKinney, *A Drop Around the World*

Steve Parker, *The Science of Water: Projects and Experiments With Water and Power*

Christine Petersen, *Water Power* (Series: True Books)

Jim Pipe, *Earthwise: Water*

Angela Royston, *The Life and Times of a Drop of Water*

Rochelle Strauss, *One Well: The Story of Water on Earth* (T)

Sally M. Walker, *Soil* (Series: Early Bird Earth Science)

Walter Wick, *A Drop of Water*

Physical Science: Forces/Simple Machines

EARLY PRIMARY/K–1

Michael Dahl, *Pull, Lift and Lower: A Book About Pulleys* (See also: *Scoop, Seesaw and Raise: A Book About Levers; Roll, Slope and Slant: A Book About Ramps; Cut, Chop and Stop: A Book About Wedges*)

Lloyd G. Douglas, *What is a Lever?*

Allan Fowler, *Simple Machines* (Series: Rookie Read-About Science)

Allan Fowler, *What Magnets Can Do*

Sally Hewitt, *Amazing Forces and Movement* (Series: Amazing Science)

Claire Llewellyn, *And Everyone Shouted "PULL!" A First Look at Forces and Motion*

Adrienne Mason, *Move It! Forces, Motion and You*

Patricia J. Murphy, *Push and Pull* (Series: Rookie Read-About Science)

LATE PRIMARY/GRADE 2–3

Kimberly Brubaker Bradley, *Forces Make Things Move*

Susan Canizares, *Simple Machines* (Series: Science Emergent Readers)

Joanna Cole, *The Magic School Bus Plays Ball: A book about forces*

Sally Hewitt, *Forces Around Us*

Sally Hewitt, *Machines We Use*

Deborah Hodge, *Simple Machines*

Claire Llewellyn, *Push and Pull* (Series: I Know That!)

Rebecca Olien, *Motion*

Chris Oxlade, *Pulleys* (Series: Simple Machines; other titles include: *Levers; Screws; Wedges; Wheels*)

Sally M. Walker, *Inclined Planes and Wedges*

Robert E. Wells, *How Do You Lift A Lion?*

Anne Welsbacher, *Levers: Understanding Simple Machines* (See also: *Pulleys; Wheels and Axels; Levers*)

INTERMEDIATE/GRADE 4–7

Michael A. DiSpezio, *Awesome Experiments: Force and Motion*

John Farndon, *Levers, Wheels and Pulleys*
Peter Lafferty, *Eyewitness: Force and Motion*
Peter D. Riley, *Forces and Movement* (Series: Staightforward Science)

Alastair Smith, *Energy, Forces and Motion* (Series: Usborne Library of Science)

Physical Science: Materials/Structure

EARLY PRIMARY/K-1

Byron Barton, *Building a House*
Sally Hewitt, *Amazing Materials* (Series: Amazing Science)
Ryan Ann Hunter, *Cross a Bridge*
Robin Nelson, *From Cement to Bridge* (Series: From Start to Finish)
Sue Tarsky, *The Busy Building Book*
Shannon Zemlicka, *From Sand to Glass* (Series: From Start to Finish)

LATE PRIMARY/GRADE 2-3

Gail Gibbons, *How a House is Built*
Bobbie Kalman, *Everyday Structures from A to Z*
Bert Kitchen, *And So They Build*

Adrienne Mason, *Build It: Structures, Systems and You*
David Evelyn Stewart, *Animal Builders*
Maxwell Newhouse, *The House That Max Built*
Philemon Sturges, *Bridges Are To Cross*

INTERMEDIATE/GRADE 4-7

Gillian Clements, *The Picture History of Great Buildings*
Clive Gifford, *Materials* (Series: Kingfisher Young Knowledge)
Etta Kaner, *Bridges*
Etta Kaner, *Towers and Tunnels*
Elaine Landau, *Bridges* (Series: True Books About Buildings and Structure; other titles include: *Tunnels; Skyscrapers; Canals*)
Bill Slavin, *Transformed: How Everyday Things Are Made*
Editors of YES magazine, *Fantastic Feats and Failures*

Physical Science: Properties of Matter

EARLY PRIMARY/K-1

Don L. Curry, *What is Mass?* (Series: Rookie Read-About Science)
Don L. Curry, *What is Matter?* (Series: Rookie Read-About Science)
Ginger Garrett, *Solids, Liquids and Gases* (Series: Rookie Read-About Science)
Tana Hoban, *Is it Rough? Is it Smooth? Is it Shiny?*

LATE PRIMARY/GRADE 2-3

Helen Frost, *Water as a Liquid* (See also: *Water as A Solid; Water as A Gas*)
Sally Hewitt, *Solid, Liquid or Gas?* (Series: It's Science!)
Adrienne Mason, *Change it! Solids, Liquids, Gases and You*
Adrienne Mason, *Touch It! Materials, Matter and You*

Ontario Science Centre, *Solids, Liquids and Gases*
Michael Elsohn Ross, *What's the Matter in Mr. Whisker's Room?*
Darlene L. Stille, *Matter: See it, Touch it, Taste it, Smell it*
Christine Webster, *Matter*
Kathleen Weidner Zoehfeld, *What is the World Made of? All About Solids, Liquids and Gases*

INTERMEDIATE/GRADE 4-7

Jacqui Bailey, *How Can Solids Be Changed?* (Series: Investigating Science)
Christopher Cooper, *Eyewitness Matter*
Alastair Smith, *Solids, Liquids and Gases* (Series: Usborne Library of Science)

Social Studies: Self/Family/Community

EARLY PRIMARY/K-1

Bobbie Kalman, *What is a Community? A–Z* (C)
Sindy McKay, *My Town* (Series: We Both Read)

Ann Morris, *Families* (Series: Around the World) (C)
Todd Parr, *The Family Book* (C)

Nuria Roca, *Your Family Tree* (Series: What Do You Know About...?)

Mari C. Schuh, *In My Town* (Series: Pebble Books: My World)

Rebecca Treays, *My Street* (Series: Young Geography) (C)

Rebecca Treays, *My Town* (Series: Young Geography) (C)

Lisa Trumbauer, *Living in a City* (Series: Communities)

LATE PRIMARY/GRADE 2-3

Heather Adamson, *A Day in the Life of a Police Officer* (Series: First Facts: Community Helpers at Work; other titles include *Day in the life of a Teacher; Day in the Life of a Veterinarian; Day in the life of a Farmer*)

Maya Ajmera, *Be My Neighbour*

Maya Ajmera, *To Be A Kid*

Paulette Bourgeois, *Fire Fighters* (Series: In My Neighborhood; other titles include: *Garbage Collectors; Postal Workers; Police Officers*)

Lisa Bullard, *My Neighbourhood: Places and Faces* (C)

Barbara Kerley, *You and Me Together: Moms, Dads and Kids Around the World* (C, T)

Bobbie Kalman, *Community Helpers A–Z* (Series: Alphabasics)

Ann Love, Canada at Work series (Titles includes: *Farming; Mining; Fishing; Forestry*)

Joan Sweeny, *Me and My Family Tree* (C)

INTERMEDIATE/GRADE 4-7

Lisa Easterling, *Families: Our Global Community*

Weigl Educational, Linking Canadian Communities series (Titles include: *Farming; Energy; Fishing; Forestry; Mining*)

Social Studies: Geography/Maps/Earth Awareness

EARLY PRIMARY/K-1

Rebecca Adburg, *Map Keys*

Neil Chesanow, *Where Do I Live?*

Allan Fowler, *North, South, East, West*

Linda Glaser, *Our Big Home* (T)

Jack Knowlton, *Maps and Globes*

Wil Mara, *The Four Oceans* (Series: Rookie Read-About Geography; other titles include *The Seven Continents*)

Bill Martin Jr., *I Love Our Earth*

Marjorie Priceman, *How To Make An Apple Pie and See the World*

Tish Rabe, *There's a Map on My Lap* (Series: Cat in the Hat Learning Library)

Marilyn Singer, *9 O'Clock Lullaby*

Joan Sweeny, *Me on the Map*

LATE PRIMARY/GRADE 2-3

Marta Segal Block, *Mapping Your Community* (Series: First Guide to Maps)

Felicity Brooks, *First Encyclopedia of Our World*

Deborah Chancellor, *Maps and Mapping*

Neil Chesanow, *Where Do I Live?*

Sara Fanelli, *My Map Book*

Gail Gibbons, *Planet Earth: Inside and Out*

Gail Hartman, *As the Crow Flies: A First Book at Maps*

Jack Knowlton, *Geography Guide from A–Z*

Bobbie Kalman, *The Earth's Oceans*

Bobbie Kalman, *Introducing Landforms*

Loreen Leedy, *Mapping Penny`s World*

Laura Ljungkvisit, *Follow the Line Around the World*

Anne Rockwell, *Our Earth*

Stacy Schuett, *Somewhere in the World Right Now*

Marilyn Singer, *On the Same Day in March: A Tour of the World's Weather*

W. Frederick Zimmerman, *The World is Flat: NOT!*

INTERMEDIATE/GRADE 4-7

Katie Daynes, *See Inside Planet Earth*

Jane P. Gardner, *The Kids Everything Geography Book*

Steve Jenkins, *Hottest, Coldest, Highest, Deepest* (T)

Briony Pénn, *The Kids Book of Canadian Geography*

Stargazer, World About Us series (Each book has text on two levels for students of mixed reading ability; titles include: *Oceans; Mountains; Rivers; Lakes*)

Social Studies: Countries and Peoples

EARLY PRIMARY/K–1

Michael Dahl, Countries Around the World series (Titles include: *Canada; China; Australia; France;* etc.)

Anne Morris, *Houses and Homes* (Series: Around the World; other titles include: *Bread, Bread, Bread; Shoes, Shoes, Shoes; Hats, Hats, Hats*)

Henry Pluckrose, *India* (Series: Picture a Country; other titles include: *Japan; Germany; China; France; Egypt*)

Rookie Read-About Geography series (Titles include: *Africa; Canada; Mexico; South America; Japan; China*)

LATE PRIMARY/GRADE 2–3

Maya Ajmera, *To Be A Kid*

Justine Fontes, *China A–Z* (Series: A-Z; other titles include: *Russia; France; Israel; Spain*)

Leila Merrell Foster, *Asia* (Series: Continents; other titles include: *North America; South America; Europe; Australia*)

Beatrice Hollyer, *Wake Up, World! A Day in the Life of Children Around the World*

Barbara Kerley, *You and Me Together: Moms, Dads and Kids Around the World*

Akira Nishivama, *Wonderful Houses Around the World*

Wendy Pfeffer, *A New Beginning: Celebrating the Spring Equinox*

TRIOS series (Three books per country: *Biography; Nonfiction; Folktale*)

Shannon Zemlicka, *Colors of China* (Series: Colors of the World)

INTERMEDIATE/GRADE 4–7

Anne Claybourne, *Usborne Book of Peoples of the World*

DK Publishing, *A Life Like Mine: How Children Live Around the World*

Miles Harvey, *Look What Came From Africa* (Series: Look What Came From…; other titles include: *Germany; China; Mexico*; etc.)

Bobbie Kalman, *Canada: The Land* (Series: Lands, Peoples, Cultures; other titles include *China; Japan; England; Spain; Peru*; etc.)

David Smith, *If the World Were a Village*

James Solheim, *It`s Disgusting and We Ate It: Food Facts From Around the World*

Social Studies: History

EARLY PRIMARY/K–1

Maria Rius, *The Middle Ages* (Series: Journey Through History)

LATE PRIMARY/GRADE 2–3

Phil Roxbee Cox, *Who Were the Romans?* (Series: Usborne Starting Points History; other titles include: *Who Built the Pyramids?; What Were Castles For?; Who Were the Vikings?*)

Sarah N. Harvey, Leslie Buffam, and Dianna Bonder, *The West Is Calling*

Betty Stroud, *The Patchwork Path: A Quilt Map to Freedom*

John The Malam, *You Wouldn't Want to Be A Roman Gladiator* (Series: You Wouldn't Want to Be…; other titles include: *A Pyramid Builder; A Medieval Knight; A Roman Soldier; A Greek Athlete*)

INTERMEDIATE/GRADE 4–7

Stephen Biesty, *Ancient World (Egypt, Rome, Greece)*

Heather Collins, *A Pioneer Story: The Daily Life of a Canadian Family in 1840*

Terry Deary, *Horrible Histories* (Series includes: *Vicious Vikings; Frightful First World War; Rotten Romans*)

Rebecca L. Grambo, *Digging Canadian History*

Carlotta Hacker, *Kids Book of Canadian History*

Andrew Langley, *The Roman News*

Deb Lucke, *The Book of Time Outs: A Mostly True History of the World's Biggest Troublemakers*

Fiona MacDonald, *I Wonder Why Greeks Built Temples And Other Questions about Ancient Greece*

Joy Masoff, *Oh Yikes! History's Grossest Moments*

Alice Schertle, *We* (T)

Peter Sis, *The Wall: Growing Up Behind the Iron Curtain*

Miranda Smith, *I Wonder Why Pyramids Were Built and other Questions About Ancient Egypt*

Valerie Wyatt, *Who Discovered America?*

Social Studies: Issues Affecting Our World

EARLY PRIMARY/K–1

Mike Artel, *Earth and Me*

Denise Fleming, *Where Once There Was A Wood* (T)

Rosie Harlow, *Garbage and Recycling: Environment Facts and Discoveries*

Scholastic First Discovery, *Endangered Animals*

LATE PRIMARY/GRADE 2–3

Jeannie Baker, *Where the Forest Meets the Sea* (T)

Melvin Berger, *Oil Spill*

Sean Callery, *I Wonder Why There's a Hole in the Sky and Other Questions About the Environment* (Series: I Wonder Why; other titles include *I Wonder Why the DoDo is Dead and other Questions about Animals in Danger*) (T)

Lynne Cherry, *The Great Kapok Tree* (T)

Nicola Davies, *Ice Bear: In the Steps of the Polar Bear* (T)

Michael Driscoll & Prof. Dennis Driscoll, *A Child's Introduction to the Environment*

Steve Jenkins, *Almost Gone* (T)

Robyn D. Friend, *A Clean Sky: The Global Warming Story*

Anne Rockwell, *Why Are the Ice Caps Melting?* (Series: Let's Read and Find Out About Science)

Paul Showers, *Where Does Garbage Go?* (Series: Let's Read and Find Out About Science)

Alexandra Wright, *Will We Miss Them?*

INTERMEDIATE/GRADE 4–7

Dr. Richard Cheel, *Global Warming Alert*

Lynne Cherry, *A River Ran Wild: An Environmental History*

Laurie David and Cambrion Gordon, *Down to Earth Guide to Global Warming*

Fred Pearce, *Earth Then and Now: Amazing Images of Our Changing World* (T)

Jack Platt, *The Vanishing Rainforest*

Rochelle Strauss, *One Well: The Story of Water on Earth* (T)

David Suzuki, *Looking at the Environment*

Jan Thornhill, *This is My Planet: The Kids Guide to Global Warming*

Social Studies: Global Citizenship

EARLY PRIMARY/K–1

Frank Asch, *The Earth and I*

Ellie Bethal, *Michael Recycle*

Nancy Elizabeth, *Recycle Every Day*

Linda Glaser, *Our Big Home* (T)

Jen Green, *Why Should I Recycle?* (See also: *Why Should I Save Water?*; *Why Should I Save Energy?*; *Why Should I Protect Nature?*)

B.J. Hennessey, *Because of You*

Alison Inches, *I Can Save the Earth! One Little Monster Learns to Reduce, Reuse, and Recycle*

Melanie Walsh, *Ten Things I Can Do to Help My World*

Rozanne Lanczak Williams, *Reduce, Reuse, Recycle* (Series: Emergent Reader Science)

LATE PRIMARY/GRADE 2–3

Alexandra Fix, *Paper* (Series: Reduce, Reuse, Recycle; other titles in the series include: *Plastic; Paper; Metal; Glass*)

Gail Gibbons, *Recycle: A Handbook for Kids*

Linda Glaser, *Our Home* (T)

Barbara Kerley, *A Little Peace* (T)

Nuria Roca, *The 3 R's: Reuse, Reduce, Re-cycle*

INTERMEDIATE/GRADE 4–7

Amanda Bishop, *How to Reduce Your Carbon Footprint*

Laurie David & Cambria Gordon, *Get Down to Earth! What You Can Do to Stop Global Warming*

Julie Hall, *A Hot Planet Needs Cool Kids*

Pearson, *Save Our Earth* (Series: Reaching Readers)

Ellen Rodger, *Building a Green Community*

Shim Schimmel, *Dear Children of the Earth*

Linda Schwartz, *Earth Book for Kids: Activities to Help Heal the Earth*

Jacquie Wines, *You Can Save the Planet*

Social Studies: Biography

Cheryl Carson, *Dr. Seuss* (Series: First Biography; other titles include *Alexander Graham Bell; Amelia Earhart; Rosa Parks*)

Dana Meachen Rau, *Neil Armstrong* (Series: Rookie Biographies; other titles include: *Laura Ingalls Wilder; George Washington; Dr. Seuss*)

Jeanette Winter, *Beatrix*

LATE PRIMARY/GRADE 2–3

David A. Adler, *A Picture Book of Jackie Robinson* (Series: Picture Book Biographies; other titles include: *Thomas Edison; Louis Braille; Amelia Earhart*)

Jo Ellen Bogart, *Emily Carr: At the Edge of the World*

Robert Coles, *The Story Of Ruby Bridges*

Carol Ghiglieri, *Helen Keller* (Series: Easy Reader Biographies; other titles include: *Martin Luther King; Alexander Graham Bell*)

Joan Holub, *Vincent Van Gogh* (Series: Smart About Art; other titles include *Pablo Picasso; Edgar Degas; Claude Monet*)

Elizabeth MacLeod, *Samuel De Champlain* (Series: Kids Can Read; other titles include: *Lucy Maud Montgomery; The Wright Brothers*)

Ainslie Manson, *Boy in Motion: Rick Hansen's Story*

Haydn Middleton, *Captain Cook: The Great Ocean Explorer* (Series: What's Their Story?; other titles include: *Cleopatra; Galileo; Gandhi; Amelia Earhart; Thomas Edison*)

Lesa Cline Ransome, *Helen Keller: The World in Her Heart*

Kathy Whitehead, *Art From Her Heart*

Jeanette Winter, *My Name is Georgia*

Jeanette Winter, *Wangari's Trees of Peace: A True Story From Africa* (T)

INTERMEDIATE/GRADE 4–7

Gerry Bailey & Karen Foster, *Cleopatra's Coin* (Series: Stories of Great People; other titles include: *Armstrong's Moon Rock; Columbus's Chart; Martin Luther King's Microphone; Leonardo's Pallet*)

Harry Black, *Canadian Scientists and Inventors*

Amy Ehrlich, *Rachel: The Story of Rachel Carson*

Christine King Farris, *My Brother Martin*

Laurie Friedman, *Angel Girl*

Nikki Giovanni, *Rosa*

Kathleen Krull, *Wilma Unlimited: How Wilma Rudolph Became the World's Fastest Woman*

Tanya Lloyd Kyl, *Canadian Boys Who Rocked the World*

Tanya Lloyd Kyl, *Canadian Girls Who Rocked the World*

Kathryn Lansky, *The Librarian Who Measured the Earth*

Kathryn Lansky, *The Man Who Made Time Travel*

Elizabeth Macleod, *Kids Book of Great Canadians*

Joanne Mattern, *Princess Diana* (Series: DK Biography)

Marc Tyler Nobel, *Boys of Steel: Creators of Superman*

Bryan Pezzi, *Terry Fox* (Series: Remarkable Canadians; other titles include: *Emily Carr; David Suzuki*)

Peter Sis, *Starry Messenger: Galileo Galilei*

Diane Stanley, *Cleopatra*

Sue Stauffacher, *Nothing but Trouble: The Story of Althea Gibson*

Maxine Trottier, *Canadian Greats* (Series includes: *Canadian Inventors; Canadian Leaders; Canadian Heroes; Canadian Explorers*)

Maxine Trottier, *Terry Fox: A Story of Hope*

Jeanette Winter, *Emily Dickinson's Letters to the World*

Jeanette Winter, *The Librarian of Basra: A True Story From Iraq*

Jane Yolen, *Encounter*

Jane Breskin Zalben, *Paths to Peace: People Who Changed the World*

Nonfiction Reading Power Instruction

I always tell teachers at my workshops that they don't really need the Nonfiction Reading Powers model, and don't really need Reading Power booklists. What is essential to the success of any comprehension instruction is their explicit teaching.

In effective literacy instruction, teachers choose the strategy to model and scaffold the students' learning by supporting and guiding the class. As students become more proficient in using the new strategies through guided practice and interaction with one another, the teacher can gradually release responsibility for the strategies to students, to encourage their independence (Pearson & Gallagher, 1983). This optimal learning model is also called the gradual release of responsibility. The ultimate goal is for students to make the strategies their own, and to know when, why, and how to apply them.

GRADUAL RELEASE OF RESPONSIBILITY

1. Teacher Modeling: "I do; you watch"

- 2–3 lessons

- explaining, demonstrating, reading aloud/thinking aloud

2. Guided Practice: "We practice together and I support you by giving tips."

- 4–6 lessons

- teacher and students practicing together in large or small groups

3. Independent Practice: "You do; I watch"

- 4–6 lessons

- students trying on their own, with monitoring; teacher may need to give more support

4. Application: "You do it on your own."

- real-life reading experiences

"Students need more structured modeling, demonstrating and coaching, and less assigning."—Allington & Cunningham (1996: 45)

When implementing the reading powers for nonfiction, strategies are initially taught in isolation. Each strategy is introduced separately and is the focus for several weeks before a new strategy is introduced. Concept lessons, teacher modeling, guided practice, and independent practice scaffold the learning for students for each of the five strategies. Depending on the grade level and students' previous experience with comprehension strategies or Reading Power, teachers may spend more or less time on each of the five reading powers. Finally, providing many opportunities to practice the strategies independently is key to successful implementation.

Teacher Modeling

"What is reading, but silent conversation."—W.S. Landor

Teacher modeling, in which the teacher is reading and thinking aloud, is one of the most effective ways for students to see strategic reading in action. We can talk about "what an active reader does" but, until we show our students what that looks like and sounds like, it is unlikely that they will be able to implement it on their own. "Talking through the text" has become common practice in many classrooms, and the active think-aloud approach is taking precedence over the more passive read-aloud.

Thinking needs to be made visible and concrete, and there are different ways to illustrate this. Sticky notes stuck directly onto the pages while you read can mark your "thinking voice." Alternatively, you can attach large white cutouts of a *Talking* bubble and a *Thinking* bubble to rulers (see templates on page 47) to hold up and indicate if your are reading with your "speaking voice" (*Talking* bubble) or explaining what your "thinking voice" is saying (*Thinking* bubble). What is essential in the modeling stage is that teachers model with purpose in mind: to demonstrate to our students that reading is an interactive process.

Explaining what you are doing and why you are doing it before you begin to read is an essential part of the modeling process:

> When a reader is reading, they have two voices: a speaking voice and a thinking voice. The speaking voice is the one that reads the words on the page that someone else wrote. The thinking voice is the voice in your head that you use to try to make sense of your reading. Today, I'm going to be reading the words from this book with my speaking voice, but then I'm going to be paying attention to my thinking while I read. When I find myself making a connection (or asking a question, or making an inference) I'm going to stop reading and tell you what I'm thinking about. This might take a little longer to read than if I was just reading the words, but I really want to show you what thinking looks like and sounds like. Most often, when you read silently, your speaking voice is quiet and you don't think out loud. But I want you to always remember—when your speaking voice is quiet, your thinking voice needs to be very loud!

Guided Practice

Guided practice is as important a step in the gradual release model, but is often not emphasized as much as modeling. Carol O'Malley, a fellow literacy mentor, shared a great analogy with me: teaching a child how to ride a bicycle using the "gradual release" model. Imagine if we taught a child to ride a bike by sitting him or her on the grass and "modeling" bike riding a few times, and then sent them off on their own. What would be the result? Instead, we spend huge amounts of time "guiding their practice": attaching training wheels to the bike, holding on to the side or back of the bike, and giving them important tips along the way—"Look straight ahead," "Keep pedaling," "Keep the bars straight," etc. When the child has learned the basics, only then do we take off the training wheels—but we still hold on to the bike. We let go only when we feel that they have mastered that balance, and often still run alongside, offering our words of encouragement and praise.

Consider your classroom. When I think of mine, I know that I have become good at the teacher modeling part of the instruction model. I think aloud all the time in classrooms, holding up that *Thinking* bubble and sharing a little insight with students. What I have not been doing as effectively, perhaps, is the guided practice. In many cases I'm sure I skipped it entirely and sent students off on their own without any extra support or guidance. Then I'd be disappointed when their work was, at best, mediocre. I now believe that it is the words of encouragement, the tips, and mini-lessons offered between the modeling and the independent practice that will really determine whether or not the independent stage will be successful. It is during these side-by-side guided lessons that I can

I have visited primary classrooms where each student has their own small *Thinking* bubble on a craft stick. During a guided read-aloud, these bubbles are used by the students to show they are thinking. As each child offers their connection or question, he or she passes the *Thinking* bubble to the teacher or place it in a basket. This enables everyone to have an opportunity to share their thinking.

Talking and Thinking Bubble Templates

Talking

Thinking

stage will be successful. It is during these side-by-side guided lessons that I can really begin to go deeper with the strategy. Mediocre results are often a result of mediocre teaching. I value the importance of the "training-wheel" lessons.

Independent Practice

Practice breeds success. With every strategy, students need many opportunities to practice the strategy on their own with texts that are at or slightly below their reading level, enabling them to focus more on their thinking than decoding. This phase of the instruction model is a good opportunity for teachers to provide more capable students the freedom to work independently, while other small groups may need extra support. While the whole class is practicing the same strategy, groups of students may be practicing with different levels of text.

Application

Our goal is for our students to be using their Nonfiction Reading Powers independently and applying them to any text. Teachers have frequently commented to me that their students, regardless of how successful they have been using the Reading Power strategies in isolation, are not taking this knowledge and applying it independently. Taking the time to explain and model application is an important stop in this instruction process.

Lesson: Using the Right Tools for Reading

- Ask students which tool a carpenter would use for putting nails in the wall. Have them come up and find the appropriate tool in the toolbox.
- Ask students how they knew which tool to use.
- Compare the box of tools to the reading brain.

> Your brain is a little like this toolbox. You have different "tools" or Reading Powers that you have learned and practiced. Depending on the book you are reading, your brain needs to find the right tool to help you understand it better. Sometimes you might need to use your Connect tool; other times, you might be in need of your Question/Infer tool. Just like a carpenter with a toolbox, it is up to you to know which tool to use to help you in the job of reading.

An anchor chart shows the reading tools students have access to.

PAY ATTENTION TO YOUR THINKING VOICE

If you find yourself saying…	you are…
"This feature tells me that…"	Zooming-In on text features
"I'm wondering about…"	Asking a Question
"Well, maybe…"	Inferring
"This reminds me of…"	Making a connection
"This sounds important."	Determining Importance
"Now, I'm thinking…"	Transforming your thinking

"The good news is that comprehension has become a long overdue reading focus. The bad news is that comprehension strategies and exercises in isolation often dominate comprehension instruction. Students are spending massive amounts of time learning and practicing these strategies, often without knowing how to apply them or not understand how they fit into the big picture of reading."—Regie Routman (2003: p.119)

For this lesson you will need a toolbox full of tools.

3 The Power to Zoom-In

"Nonfiction is one of the most accessible genres for reluctant and less experienced readers because the features scaffold the reader's understanding."—Stephanie Harvey and Anne Goudvis (2000: 120)

A Grade 8 class is given comprehension assessment based on a passage of nonfiction text. This passage includes several nonfiction features such as charts, captions, and diagrams. Most of the questions the students are asked are based on the features in the text, rather than the main body of text. The result: a majority of students failed to answer questions correctly.

These students did what I may have done in Grade 8—skip over the features and read only the main body of the text. Because I read mostly fiction, my eyes automatically gravitate to the type of text with which I am most familiar. I thought the other stuff on the page was more decorative than important. It may not be as obvious to some readers that text features are signals for the reader to stop and pay attention. Students need to be introduced to nonfiction features and their purpose if they are to learn to read information effectively.

Nonfiction texts vary in many ways from fiction, but most significantly in the structure of the text and the way the information is presented. Information is found in many places on the page of a nonfiction text, and is presented in a variety of ways: on a graph or in a chart, highlighted in a fact box or featured as a caption under a photograph. These features can help readers navigate through the text, summarize key points, highlight important information, and provide a variety of ways a reader can access the information. In this technological age, young readers are experienced with navigating through a web page by clicking on icons to access more information. The printed page, however, is not as interactive as a web page, and readers need to learn to use their eyes the way they use their mouse, focusing on the features to access information.

It may be that your district or your school uses different terminology to describe what I'm referring to as text features, such as *nonfiction conventions*. As long as the term being used is consistent within your school, it will not make a difference to these lessons.

In determining the reading strategies to help students read information more effectively, we need to first introduce a general awareness of the structure and features of the genre so that students can learn how to use them effectively when learning and practicing the subsequent reading strategies. Just as a camera has the ability to "zoom in" or highlight a portion of an image, readers can learn to Zoom-In on the features of a nonfiction text to highlight what is important. Teaching students what nonfiction features are, why they are important, and how to recognize and interpret them is an important part of helping students make sense of informational texts. Nonfiction Features

- help the reader locate information more easily
- organize the information to make it easier to read
- often highlight or restate important information
- make the information easier to read or access

Introducing the Power to Zoom-In

For this lesson you will need
- a Primary resource: e.g., *A Closer Look* by Mary McCarthy; *Looking Down* by Steve Jenkins (works for intermediate, too); *Looking Closely Through the Forest* by Frank Serafini (or any of Serafini's *Looking Closely* series)

or
- an Intermediate resource: e.g., *Zoom* or *Re-Zoom* by Istvan Banyai
- the Nonfiction Reading Powers model (page 29)

While adults may take it for granted that students understand the expression "zoom in," it is worth taking the time to ensure that they know what it means.

- Begin the lesson:

  I have a book that I'm going to share with you today. It is a picture book with no words. I'm not going to tell you too much more about it, but I would like you to look carefully at the pictures while I turn the pages and then we'll share our thinking about the book.

- Begin to "read" the book, turning the pages slowly so that the students have time to observe. Ask students to turn and talk to a partner about what they notice is happening in the book.
- Share another similar book, and then ask students to share what they notice is the same in the second book.
- Write *Zoom-In* on the board or overhead and ask if anyone knows what it means. Discuss the concept and make reference to a camera and the difference between a close-up picture and a long shot.
- Ask how the books you just shared reflect Zooming-In.
- End the lesson:

  Today I wanted to introduce you to the reading power of Zooming-In, or getting a closer look at something.

  (Place *Zoom-In* puzzle piece in head of Nonfiction Reading Powers model.)

  For the next while, we are going to be zooming-in on pages of nonfiction texts. Nonfiction books have a lot going on on each page. Active readers are able to zoom-in on certain places on the page to find the information that they need. When you zoom-in, it means you take a closer look at some certain parts of the page, instead of skipping over them. Zooming-in helps you to focus on information you are trying to find or that is important.

Books for Zooming-In

Istvan Banyai, *Zoom* (I)

Lucy & Meg Clibbon, Imagine You're a… series
   (Includes: *Imagine You're a Wizard; Pirate; Knight; Princess; Fairy*) (P)

DK Publishing, EYE Know series (P)

Franklin Watt Publishing, Cycles of Life series
   (Includes: *Animal Builders; Pond Life Seasons; Growing Things; Hibernation*) (P)

Margaret Frith and others, Smart About Art Series
   (Includes: *Vincent Van Gogh; Frieda Kahlo; Edgar Degas*) (I)

Deborah Hodge, *Ants* (P)

Steve Jenkins, *On Top of the World* (I)
Istvan Banyai, *Re-Zoom* (I)
Steve Jenkins, *Looking Down* (P)
Editors of Kingfisher, *Creepy Crawlies* (Series: Question Time) (I)
Mary McCarthy, *A Closer Look* (P)
National Geographic KIDS, Science Readers series
Nelson, Focus series
Pearson, Reaching Readers series

Scholastic, GO Facts series (Reading levels from Emergent to Grade 3) (P)
Frank Serafini, *Looking Closely Through the Forest* (Series: Looking Closely)
Editors of TIME For Kids, TIME For Kids books
Whitecap Books, Investigate series (I)
Wright Group, Take Two Books series (Paired books, one fiction and one nonfiction; various reading levels and Big Book sets)

Scaffolded Lessons for Zooming-In

Lesson 1 (Teacher Directed/Guided Practice): Comparing Fiction and Nonfiction

Pairing fiction and nonfiction books on the same topic and comparing them visually is an effective way of helping students zoom-in on the nonfiction features. As important as noticing the nonfiction features (conventions) is the reflection at the end of the lesson on the purpose of the features.

- Begin the lesson:

  I have two books to show you today. I would like you to look carefully at the covers of each and tell me which one you think is fiction and which one is nonfiction.

- You can start to create your own list, or just do the lesson orally. Most students will be able to tell which is which, but it is important that they are also able to tell you how they know. Possible answers:
  - titles might be different
  - photographs vs. illustration
  - name of author and illustrator on cover vs. name of author only

  Now let's look inside at the first page of each book. I'd like you to Zoom-in and tell me what you notice. What is the same and what is different?

  (Often the first page of each is the title page; the visuals may be different.)

  Let's see the next page. Oh, look… This book (fiction) has the title again but no illustrations. But over here (nonfiction book) I see something totally different (table of contents). Does anybody know what this is called? Does anybody know what it's for?

  The next page is the start of each book. Both pages have a page number on them. I'm noticing this book (fiction) has an illustration here and the words of the

For this lesson you will need
- a pair of books, one fiction and one nonfiction, on the same topic: *All About Spiders* (Kingfisher) and *The Very Busy Spider* by Eric Carle

Try to use a nonfiction book that includes a lot of text features. Avoid nonfiction books that have a layout similar to a fiction book; i.e., a visual on the top of the page and a sentence underneath.

I like the Take Two Books (published by the Wright Group): a series of books that come in sets, or pairs. One is a fiction and the other is a nonfiction, but both are on the same topic. They also come in Big Book form, making the modeling lessons more effective.

story are here. In this (nonfiction) book, however, I'm noticing lots of things going on. The first thing I notice is the way the page is laid out. It's different than the other book—the page is broken up into different sections. I'm noticing that there are different kinds of printing on the page—here the printing is big and bold, down here is smaller, over here there are words that appear darker. I wonder why the printing is different. I'm also noticing the photographs rather than illustrations. And under this picture there is a separate sentence telling about this picture.

- Continue modeling in this way, "noticing" the similarities and differences.
- Give a pair of books (one fiction and one nonfiction) to a pair of students. Invite them to look through their books together, page by page, and "point and talk" to their partner, noticing what is the same and what is different in the two books.
- End the lesson: Gather the class together and reflect on what they have learned. (I use big books for this part of the lesson). It is important to lead them into a discussion of the purpose of nonfiction features.

So let's talk about your fiction and nonfiction books. What are some things you noticed about the two books?

(Allow time for several responses)

One of the things we've noticed about nonfiction books is how the pages look different from the pages of a fiction book. A fiction book might have words and a picture, but a page of a nonfiction book can have many different things: charts, photographs, maps, bold headings, labels.

(Hold up a nonfiction book and point to the features)

All of these things we see in nonfiction books have a special name: we call them "nonfiction features." They are characteristics of nonfiction books, and most nonfiction books include some of them. Fiction books, as you can see, do not have these features.

(Hold up a fiction book and turn several pages)

Now, I would like you to take a moment to think about why that might be. Why do nonfiction books have these special features, but fiction books do not? Please talk to your elbow partner about this.

- Allow time for discussion and then have students share. Recap and record their answers on chart paper (the result might resemble the boxed text on page 54).

In the next couple of weeks, we are going to spend some time really getting to know all the different kinds of nonfiction features. But the most important thing I want you to remember is that those features are there to help you.

Grade 3 teachers at South Poplar Elementary School pass out leftover Scholastic Book Club flyers to their students for a creative cut-and-sort lesson. Students use the titles and covers as clues to distinguish between fiction and nonfiction books.

Lesson 2 (Teacher Directed/Independent Practice): Creating a Venn Diagram

For this lesson you will need
- chart paper or a SMART board with a Venn diagram drawn on it

Students will need
- copies of Venn Diagram (page 59) and Cut and Sort (page 58) for independent work

- Begin the lesson:

  Yesterday we looked at the similarities and differences between a fiction and a nonfiction text. We also learned about text features. Today we are going to use that information and organize it into this Venn diagram.

Label the circles at the top: *Fiction* and *Nonfiction*.

- Model one or two concepts; e.g., *Story* and *Fact*; *Imagination* and *Information*.
- Ask the students to brainstorm some of the similarities and differences, adding to the chart as they respond.
- After a few responses, students can work in pairs to complete their own Venn diagrams (use Venn Diagram, page 59). Depending on the grade level, students might need the Cut and Sort labels (page 58) to glue onto their Venn diagrams.

Lesson 3 (Teacher Directed/Independent Practice): Nonfiction Feature Search

This lesson allows children to search through various nonfiction books to locate different features. It helps them become familiar with the vocabulary associated with the features and see the variety of ways information can be represented.

For this lesson you will need
- a selection of nonfiction books that include lots of text features

Students will need
- copies of Nonfiction Feature Search (pages 60–61) for independent work

- Begin the lesson:

  Who can tell me the names of some nonfiction features that you may find in a nonfiction text?

  (List on chart paper as students respond, or create a full-page chart that includes sketches.)

  Today you are going to go on a search for some of these features to see how many you can find.

It is important to explain to primary students that they are searching for the feature and not the specific illustration or map on their sheet. I have the experience of students searching for "the turtle" rather than the caption.

  (Pass out copies of Nonfiction Feature Search, pages 60–61.)

- In pairs, students choose a nonfiction book to search. Make sure that the books the children are using include many of the features. Students go through and identify the text features in their book.

Lesson 4 (Teacher Directed/Independent Practice): Creating a Nonfiction Feature Dictionary

Having students create a dictionary of nonfiction features is a way of reinforcing language and vocabulary, as well as helping them you see how features can represent information in a different way.

For this lesson you will need
- chart paper for brainstorming
- pre-made blank booklets made from folded and stapled 8.5" x 14" white paper

- Begin the lesson:

  Who can tell me the names of some text features we might find in a nonfiction book? (Record responses on chart paper; you can include a quick visual beside each notation.)

This lesson is adapted from *Strategies That Work* (Harvey & Goudvis, 2007: 122–124).

Nonfiction Text Features

Web	Map	Title
Caption	Fact box	Headings
Venn diagram	Sidebar	Italics/Bold print
Linear chart	Labels	Diagram
Flow chart	Comparison	Photograph
Table of contents	Index	Glossary

• Decide if each student will create an individual dictionary, or if the class will collaborate to create one dictionary.

INDIVIDUAL DICTIONARY

• Fold three sheets of blank 8.5" x 14" paper in half; staple them together at the crease to create a six-page booklet.
• Give each student a blank booklet.
• Each student chooses 5 or 6 features to include in his or her dictionary. (See possible choices above). Each dictionary page must include:
  • the name of the feature at the top of the page
  • the page number where an example can be found
  • a drawn and colored example of the text feature

Students can choose the context for the feature, and features do not need to be connected in any way. I usually make the Table of Contents a required feature.

CLASS DICTIONARY

• Have students pair up.
• Each pair of students creates one dictionary page, focusing on one nonfiction feature.
• Collect all the pages to create a class dictionary of nonfiction features.

To ensure that we don't end up with a dictionary that includes 15 pages on captions, I make sure that every pair of students has a different feature to work on.

Dictionary of Nonfiction Features: samples of Web and Fact Box

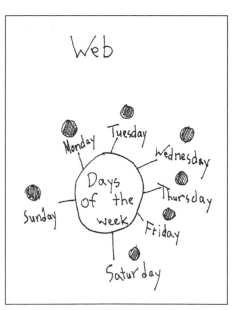

Dictionary of Nonfiction Features: samples of Labels and Close ups

Lesson 5 (Teacher Directed/Guided Practice): Seymour Simon Needs our Help!

During my extensive search for nonfiction books for children, I became familiar with many nonfiction authors. Seymour Simon was one of those authors I got to know very well because, no matter where on the library shelf you go, you will find a Seymour Simon book. A highly acclaimed science writer for children, he has written books on every land animal, sea creature, planet, body part, natural disaster. His bibliographical listings are in the hundreds, his topics are appealing to children, and his photography is extraordinary. But for one reason, and one reason only, I avoided purchasing any of Seymour Simon's books for my classroom. Seymour Simon does not include ANY text features in his books: no table of contents, no headings, no diagrams or captions, not even a page number! As much as I love to look at the photography, even I find his books challenging to read. But his books are great for showing students the importance of text features.

For this lesson you will need
• several copies of books by Seymour Simon
• an overhead transparency of one page from a Seymour Simon book: e.g., *Animals Nobody Loves* for Intermediate; SeeMORE readers for Primary

This lesson is for students Grade 3 and up.

• Begin the lesson:

Today I'd like to introduce you to an author of nonfiction science books; his name is Seymour Simon. Seymour Simon has written more than 200 nonfiction books for children: books on animals, sea creatures, sharks, gorillas, planets, the human body, the sun, the moon, earthquakes, tornadoes—you name it and Seymour Simon has written a book about it. One thing I love about Seymour Simon books is that they are full of beautiful and extraordinary photographs.

(Hold up some of the covers)

But there is one thing about Seymour Simon's books that bothers me a little. And maybe the best way to discuss this with you is to show you some of his books and see if you can figure it out.

(Open up book and show the pages and pages of text to the students.)

The discovery of pages and pages of text with no text features has, on many occasions, produced a collective gasp. Having spent several previous lessons on nonfiction features, students quickly notice when they are not included.

- Ask students to turn and talk to their elbow partners about what they notice and how that might affect their reading. Allow time for sharing and discussion.
- Continue the lesson:

I'm thinking that reading a book like this might make it much harder for me as a reader. If I want to find out what gorillas eat, for example, I need to start at the beginning and read every page before I can find information on diet. So what does that tell me about the importance of nonfiction features? It tells me that they really help the reader by sorting out the information and organizing it in a way that makes it easier to read. Today, we're going to help Seymour Simon by creating some nonfiction features for his books.

- Model this with the class. Make an overhead transparency of one of the pages and read the piece out loud to the students.

There is a lot of information on this page, but no features. Can you think of a feature we could add to this page to help the reader find the information more easily? Talk to your elbow partner to come up with ideas.

- Have students brainstorm different features and model on the overhead some quick sketches of text features, such as a caption, a heading, or a fact box.
- Pass out copies of several pages from Seymour Simon books.
- Students, in pairs, design one or two text features for each page to "help Seymour."
- Application: For anyone who, like me, has been assigning the five-paragraph animal research report year after year, the study of nonfiction features can certainly add variety and some exciting extensions to an often dull final project. Rather than having my students simply write out five paragraphs, they are now required to include at least three different nonfiction features to their report. Representing new learning through text features encourages students to synthesize the information and present it in different ways.

Sample of Text Feature *Comparison* using *Baby Animals* by Seymour Simon.

Lesson 6 (Teacher Directed/Independent Practice): Text Features with Lucy and Meg Books

For this lesson you will need
• copies of books by Lucy and Meg Clibbon: e.g., *Imagine You're a Pirate, Imagine You're a Wizard, Imagine You're a Mermaid*
Students will need
• Text Features sheet (page 62)

This lesson is for early primary students.

Text Features: Kindergarten sample of labels on *Imagine You're a Pirate* by Meg Clibbon.

Heather Rose, Literacy Helping Teacher in Penticton, BC, uses the Lucy and Meg books to model text features to early primary students. Students learn about titles, labels, and captions from these colorful, humorous books.

• Begin the lesson: Read aloud several pages from one of the Lucy and Meg books, focusing on the pages that display prominent text features (the first five pages).
• Explain to students that they're going to create their own page modeled after the book, including text features of labeling, title, and caption.
• Students draw a character of their choice (either one from the book or a different one) and add labels, bold headings, and a caption.

Lesson 7 (Guided and Independent Practice): Creating Body Maps

For this lesson you will need
• *My Map Book* by Sara Fanelli
• large sheets of paper (long enough to trace students' whole bodies)

The same book has been the inspiration for many other creative activities and writing extensions, including "Map of my Heart" for Valentines Day.

Teacher Gillian Partridge shared this creative lesson with me. She uses the book as inspiration for other creative activities and writing extensions, including "Map of My Heart" for Valentines Day.

• Begin the lesson: Have students brainstorm their summer holidays, focusing on their senses and related parts of the body:
  • what I saw
  • what I heard
  • what I tasted
  • what I smelled
  • where I walked
  • what I felt with my hands
  • what I felt with my heart
  • what I thought about
• Each students lies on a piece of paper while a partner traces around the outline of his/her body, including hands and feet.
• Students color in the details of their body maps. Enlarged photos of the students' faces can be glued on to the heads.
• Using the brainstormed list, students create labels to glue on or near the corresponding body part on their life-size replica.

Cut and Sort

Not true	Dialogue; e.g., "Hi," he said.	Facts and Information
Title Page	Page Numbers	Venn Diagram
Titles and Headings	Characters	You can start reading anywhere
Setting	Photographs	Story
Charts and graphs	Illustrations	Table of Contents
Fact Boxes	**Bold Print**, *Italics*	Headings
Beginning–Middle–End	You have to start at the beginning	Comparisons
Text Structure	Problem–Solution	Maps
Index	Not a story	Glossary
"Once upon a time…"	Captions	Imagination
Real people and places	Labels	Fairy Tale

Venn Diagram

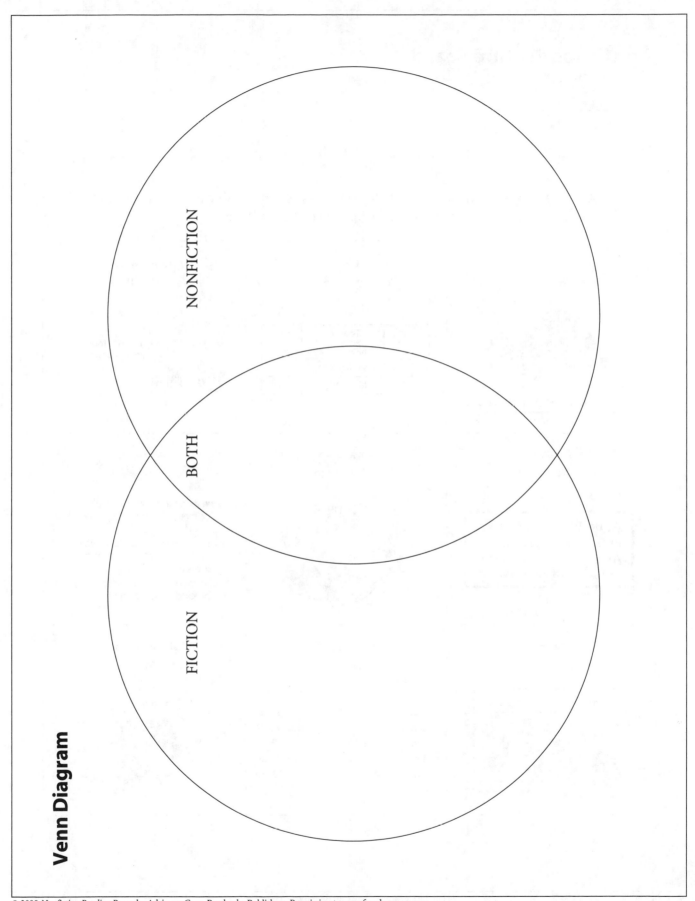

NONFICTION

BOTH

FICTION

Nonfiction Feature Search

Name: _____

Title: _____   Author: _____

Skim through the book and find as many of these features as you can. Circle "Yes" or "No" to tell if you found the feature; write in the page number where the feature is found.

Caption	**Chart**	**Comparison**
Yes No Page___	Yes No Page___	Yes No Page___

Caption

Yes   No   Page___

The turtle has a hard shell.

Chart

Yes   No   Page___

Grade	Teacher	Room
4	Mrs. Jones	24
5	Mr. Nguyen	40
6	Miss Singh	12

Comparison

Yes   No   Page___

A T-Rex's tooth is the size of a corn cob.

Fact Box

Yes   No   Page___

A **deciduous** tree loses its leaves in the winter. An **evergreen** tree keeps its leaves all year.

Flow Chart

Yes   No   Page___

Glossary

Yes   No   Page___

artery: a blood vessel that conveys blood away from the heart

capillary: a minute blood vessel that connects the arteries to the veins

vein: a blood vessel that conveys blood to the heart

Graph

Yes   No   Page___

Index

Yes   No   Page___

den   8, 22
giraffe   15, 18, 20
hyena   9, 21
jungle   4, 12, 24-26
lion   23, 30

Labeled Diagram

Yes   No   Page___

apple
pear
banana
plum

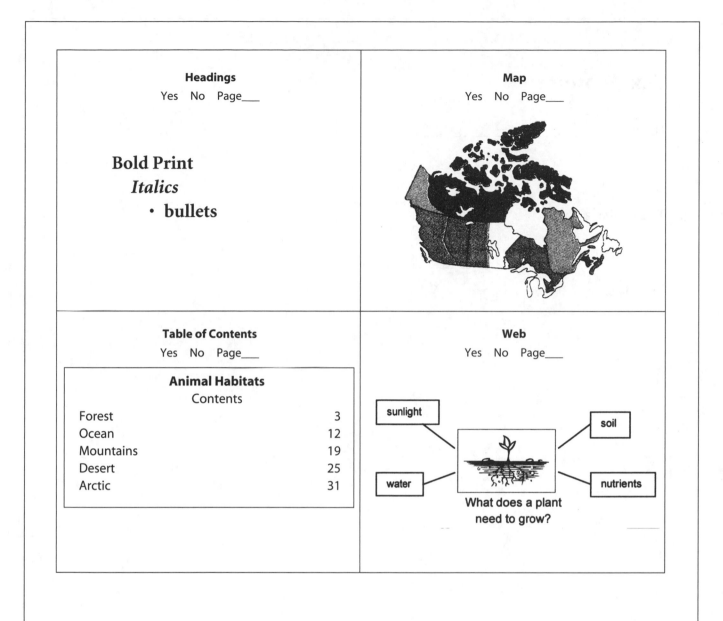

Headings

Yes   No   Page___

Bold Print
Italics
• bullets

Map

Yes   No   Page___

Table of Contents

Yes   No   Page___

Animal Habitats
Contents

Forest	3
Ocean	12
Mountains	19
Desert	25
Arctic	31

Web

Yes   No   Page___

sunlight

soil

water

nutrients

What does a plant
need to grow?

Text Features

Name: _____

This is what a

_____

looks like.

Everyone knows what a

_____

looks like.

4 The Power to Question/Infer

When I was a student, the majority of questions being asked in classrooms came from the teacher. As an obedient, albeit keen, student, I knew my role was to answer the questions that the teacher asked. A question, in my experience, had either a right or a wrong answer. My goal was to ensure that the answer I gave was always the right one. The source for all correct answers, I believed, lay within the literal contours of a text. If I could not find the answers there, I was incapable of answering them.

Reading in my class was working through an SRA kit—that wonderful compact neatly-organized box filled with shiny color-coded cards. Each card had a narrow black-and-white drawing at the top and the story below, followed by ten questions on the back. The stories were leveled by colors and we worked our way methodically through each of the stories of one color and then moved into the next set of colors. If my memory serves me correctly, the colors at the front of the box, at the lowest reading level, were muddy tones with rather unpleasant names: tan, rust, gray, mustard. The colors toward the back of the box were far more appealing: magenta, aquamarine, goldenrod. SRA kits reinforced all my beliefs about questions: read the question, and find the correct answer within the text. The actual process of reading the SRA card was frequently skipped, a time-saving strategy used by many—after all, why bother reading when you could find all the answers directly in the text? Often, I had no idea what the story was about, yet managed to answer the questions correctly. There were exceptions, however: those few questions that required the reader to actually think. It was those inferential questions that prevented me from moving up to goldenrod and aquamarine. So there I remained, stuck in the mustard, because I hadn't been taught how to think.

Reflecting on my own classroom experience, I realize that, by not being encouraged to ask questions, and by being conditioned to answer primarily literal questions, what I had lost was confidence in my own thinking. Encouraging questions and deep explorations into our thinking results in a confidence within ourselves: *my* questions and *my* thinking matters. Questions not only help us better understand text, they help us better understand the world. Questions propel us forward, moving us from a passive stance into an active stance. Questions lead readers into the text and enable them to interact and find meaning. We ask questions *before* we read to set purpose, *while* we read to clarify content and determine the author's intent, and *after* we read to extend our understanding. When reading information books, we ask questions to guide our reading, which is why it is an important strategy to teach early in the process.

Many would agree that teacher-generated questions dominate classrooms. Children often have difficulty generating questions because they become so accustomed to answering rather than asking. One teacher told me the story of a lesson she was doing on questioning with her Grade 1 class. Rather than generating questions, the students continued to tell facts about spiders. The teacher stopped, explaining to the students that she wanted them to *ask the questions*, reminding them that a question usually began with a "who," "what," "where," "when," or "why." She asked if anyone had a question about spiders that began with a *w* sound. One little boy put up his hand and said, "WELLLL, I saw a spider once in my bathtub!"

In their book *Creating the Curious Classroom*, Rod Peterson and Les Asselstine discuss how classrooms that value student-centred inquiry develop communities of learners who understand that thinking is a way to understand the world. As with the other reading powers in this book, questioning is not a way of reading, it is a way of thinking and living. Classrooms that resonate with questions are cultivating thinking. I want my students to question me, question the text, question each other, and question the world. From these questions can emerge the most meaningful learning experiences and activities. Curriculum, with input of student inquiry, promotes engagement. Units of study in science, math, and social studies that begin with the students' questions set the stage for thinking and learning.

Rachel Carson (1998) believes that children are naturally curious. As they grown and learn, they question the world around them. How many questions they ask and how long they keep asking is dependent on how their questions are being valued. My goal, when teaching this strategy to students, is to have their questions fill the classroom and become the catalyst for learning in all subject areas, not just reading.

Linking Questioning and Inferring

Inferring is a strategy that is often introduced and taught separately, as I did in my previous book *Reading Power*. Stephanie Harvey and Anne Goudvis see a strong link between the strategies of visualizing and inferring, and have put them together into one chapter of their book. In my learning and reflecting on these strategies, I have seen a more prominent link between the powers of questioning and inferring. Questions that require the reader to think beyond a literal understanding are a direct pathway to inferring. When an answer can not be found within the confines of the text, readers must infer, or add their thinking into the text, to fill in what is not there with their own ideas. Questions lead directly to inferences.

Regardless of the genre, structure, or context of a piece of text, a writer cannot possibly supply every detail or piece of information. Active readers are aware of this and will read with the intent of adding their own ideas into the text. For many adult readers, we may not be aware that we are "adding" our thinking into the text: our ideas flow in and out of the text undetected, and we remain unaware that we are inferring.

In this chapter, we begin with lessons that promote deep-thinking questioning in all aspects of learning, then bridge the strategy with lessons that move students from their questions into inferring. Pictures are used initially to stimulate and encourage questions. Once the students gain understanding of the thinking process involved in both strategies, we move forward into text.

"Children are born curious. They look at the world around them and ask why, how? Unfortunately, what is second nature to our toddlers and primary-grade students often dissipates as they move into the intermediate grades. Although many of our students become relatively proficient at answering teacher-generated questions, they forget the most important questions—their own."—Michelle Kelley and Nicki Clausen-Grace (2007: 118)

Quick Questions	Deep-Thinking Questions
• Quick to answer	• Takes more time to answer (deep-thinking pose)
• Answer found in the book	• Answer not in the text; from another source (another book or your thinking)
• Usually one correct answer	• Often not one correct answer
• Helps to clarify content	• Helps to deepen understanding
• Once you know the answer, your thinking stops	• Because you don't know the answer, your thinking keeps going

I often invite the students to first find their "deep-thinking pose." I can often tell when people are thinking deeply because they *look* like they are thinking.

Introducing the Power to Question

When introducing this strategy, I spend time immersing the students into asking questions by introducing the concept of quick and deep-thinking questions.

For this lesson you will need
• the Nonfiction Reading Powers model (page 29)

• Begin the lesson:

Active readers ask questions before, during, and after they read. Questioning leads the reader deeper into the text and encourages thinking. There are two different kinds of questions you might ask when you are reading. One is called a "quick" question. A quick question is one that you ask and, as you keep reading, you find the answer in the book. You might wonder if the boy will ever find his lost hockey stick, and then at the end of the story, you find out that he did. With a quick question, after you find the answer, you don't need to keep thinking about it—your thinking stops.

The other kind of question a reader may ask is called a "deep-thinking" question. This is also a question you ask while you are reading, but when you finish reading, you still don't know the answer. If you never find out the answer, then you need to answer it by thinking. With deep-thinking questions, your thinking keeps on going.

If information books do not contain the answer to our questions, we can continue our search by looking at other sources, such as another book or a website.

• Create an anchor chart like the above, to keep in the room for reference.
• Practice asking children quick and deep-thinking questions so that they can begin to recognize the difference.

I'm going to ask you some quick questions. As soon as you know the answer, you may say it out loud: What's your name? How old are you? What school do you go to? What's the principal's name? How many brothers do you have? What day is it today?

(After the quick questions, reflect with the students)

What did you notice about those questions? (They were easy) Were they quick to answer? (Yes) Why? (Because we didn't have to think about them) What happened to your thinking? (It stopped as soon as we answered)

Now I'm going to ask you a different type of question—a deep-thinking question. I'd like you to notice what happens to your thinking when I ask this question.

Here is my question for you: I was in my car the other day, waiting at a stop light, and I glanced beside me and noticed the man in the car beside mine was yawning. It was ten o'clock in the morning, and I wasn't tired, but seeing the man yawn made me yawn too. So I was wondering, why does that happen? When I see someone sneeze, it doesn't make me sneeze, but when I see someone yawn it makes me yawn. I would like you to think about that for a while—in your deep-thinking pose.

(Allow time for thinking)

Now share your thinking with your partner.

- Emphasize that the answer to your question is not important. What *is* important is that students experience the process of "deep-thinking questions," questions that encourage us to explore our thinking.
- Extend the lesson: There are many books for promoting the notion of deep-thinking questions that I introduce during these first lessons (see box). Many of them have writing extensions that encourage students to explore their own deep-thinking questions. They can be springboards for effective writing extensions.

Books for Deep-Thinking Questions

While I recognize that some of these books are fiction, my goal for these initial lessons is to teach and encourage questioning as a way for readers to get a sense of not only texts, but also of themselves and of the world around them.

P = primary
I = Intermediate

Connie Amarel, *I Wonder Why: A Poem for Children* (P)

Jim Bruce, *What? Where? Why? Questions and Answers About Nature* (I)

Philip Cam (editor), *Thinking Stories 1, 2 & 3* (The Children's Philosophy Series) (P, I)

Antje Damm, *Ask Me* (P)

Harriet Fishel, *I Wonder* (P)

Marie Louise Gay, Stella books (P)

Ian James, *Biggest Ever Books of Questions and Answers* (I)

Steve Jenkins, *Looking Down* (P, I)

Tana Hoban, *I Wonder* (P)

Sarah Perry, *If* (P, I)

Christopher Phillips, *The Philosopher's Club* (I)

Lila Prap, *Why?* (P)

Brigitte Raab, *Where Does Pepper Come From?* (P)

Catherine Ripley, *Why? Everyday Questions About Science, Nature and the World Around You* (P, I)

Lois Rock, *I Wonder Why* (P)

Gregory Stock, *The Kids Book of Questions* (revised edition) (I)

David A. White, *Philosophy for Kids: 40 Fun Questions That Help You Wonder About Everything!* (I)

Kathy Wollard, *How Come? Planet Earth* (I)

Scaffolded Lessons for Questioning

Lesson 1 (Teacher Directed): Wonder Objects

For this lesson you will need
- a special object that has a story behind it

In her book *Comprehension Connections*, Tanny McGregor (2007: 63–65) describes how she introduces the strategy of questioning to her students using the Questioning Rock. This lesson is to encourage questioning.
- Begin the lesson:

   I've brought in this special object from home today. I'm not going to tell you very much about it right now, only that it is very special to me. I'd like to pass it around and let you hold it and examine it.

- Pass object around, allowing students to examine it.
- Invite students to ask questions about the object:

   What are you wondering about this object?

- Record student answers on chart paper.
- Keep the object on display in the room, and invite students to write any new questions they have.
- Each day, during morning gathering, reveal a little information about your object. Invite students to ask more questions as they learn more about the object.
- Extend the lesson: Each week, one student brings in a "special object" to share, display, and tell the story behind it. Discourage objects such as toys, collectible cards, and sport trophies; encourage students to bring in unique objects that have unique stories behind them.

Lesson 2 (Teacher Directed/Independent Practice): Wander and Wonder

For this lesson you will need
- *I Wonder* by Tana Hoban

Each student will need
- an inexpensive magnifying glass
- a science notebook and a pencil

Science journaling or notebooking has become prevalent in science education. With this approach, there is a greater emphasis on developing students' abilities in communicating scientific understanding. These science notebooks have open-ended formats for students to record questions they have, record observations, make scientific drawings, etc. This lesson encourages scientific inquiry, and works particularly well as you launch into a new science unit.
- Begin the lesson: Read aloud *I Wonder* by Tana Hoban.

   I chose this book to read today because it is all about questions. We've been talking about questions and how asking questions helps to deepen our understanding. Today we are going to go on a scientific exploration, and we are going to record our wonderings.

Science Notebooks – Writing About Inquiry by Brian Campbell and Lori Fulton (2003) is a great resource for anyone interested in exploring this inquiry approach to science.

- Explain to students that their science notebooks are Wonder Notebooks.
- Pass out notebooks and magnifying glasses to students.
- Take students to the nearest park or an area of trees in the schoolyard.
- Demonstrate how to use the magnifying glass to find a small space to study.
- Explain to students they are going to examine a small area through the magnifying glass, and that they are to wonder about what they see there.
- Model questions:

I wonder how these cracks formed in the tree? I wonder why this moss is on this side but not over here? I wonder where this little ant is going and what it's doing?

- Open your Wonder Notebook and model how to draw a close-up diagram and use labels to record questions.
- Invite students to find a small nature space, study the space with the magnifying glass, and record their findings in their Wonder Notebooks.

Teacher model of close-up drawing of a section of tree trunk, labeled with questions.

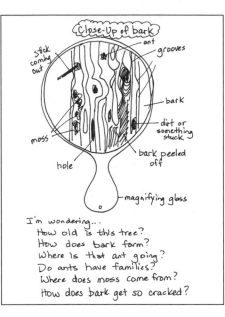

Lesson 3 (Independent Practice): Wonder Webs

Wonder Webs are an effective way of helping students generate questions on a specific topic. They can be used at the beginning of a new science or social studies unit. When the unit begins with students' questions, they take ownership and become more engaged.

For this lesson you will need
- chart paper or SMART board for modeling

For this lesson each student will need
- a My Wonder Web template (page 71)

- Begin the Lesson: Introduce the new unit of study to the students.
- Have students brainstorm with a partner things that they already know about the topic.
- Have students think about things that they are wondering about the topic, things they are interested in finding out.
- On chart paper, begin to create a web of questions that the students share.
- Pass out My Wonder Web and have students work independently, filling out the web with their own questions about the topic.
- At the end of your unit of study, it is important for students to return to their Wonder Webs and reflect on their questions.

If your unit of study is very broad, such as Weather, encourage students to narrow their focus for their Wonder Web to a more specific topic, such as Wind or Rain.

Wonder Web: Grade 2 sample on "What I'm wondering about Wind."

My Wonder Web

how can Wind carry stuff?

das Wind Kam fnom air?

is there Wind in outer space?

What maks the Wind?

Wind

how fast can it go?

how heavy is it?

Lesson 4 (Teacher Directed/Guided Practice): Questions and Discoveries

For this lesson each student will need
• Questions and Discoveries sheet (page 72)

One of the purposes of asking questions is to extend our learning and gain new information. Teachers Janice Novakowski and Laura Birarda use this lesson as a way to launch into a unit of study.
• Begin the lesson: Spend some time discussing and recording students' background knowledge about the topic of the unit of study.
  Here's what we already know or think we know about _____.

• Invite students to ask questions about the topic:

  Here's what we don't know but we are wondering about.

• Record these inquiry questions on a chart as a reference.
• As a class, discuss ways the students might find answers to their questions: books, the Internet, asking an expert, observing.
• Have each student choose two related questions to pursue. Students record their questions and discoveries on the Questions and Discoveries form on page 72. Beginning with a question gives the students a purpose for reading.
• Extend the lesson: Students later share their discoveries and learning with the class. End the unit of study by revisiting the original chart of questions, celebrating their new knowledge, and reflecting on how questions can lead to new discoveries.

Lesson 5 (Teacher Directed): Practicing Quick and Deep-Thinking Questions with Texts

For this lesson you will need
• any nonfiction text

While many of the preceding lessons focus on generating deep-thinking questions, it is important to give students practice in answering all questions. This strategy reinforces the difference between quick and deep-thinking questions, and gives students practice in asking and answering both.

• Begin the lesson: Review the different types of questions; i.e., quick vs. deep-thinking.

- Invite one student volunteer to come to the front and model the strategy with you.

  Today we're going to practice reading a chunk of text and asking each other questions about it. Some of the questions will be *quick*—we will be able to find the answers right in the text. Some questions will be *deep-thinking*—we will need to use our thinking to answer them.

- Explain that the student is going to be reading a chunk of text aloud. Then you will be asking three questions about the text: two quick questions and one deep-thinking question.
- Ask student to read aloud a piece of text you have marked.
- Ask two quick questions; student finds the answer in the text.
- Ask a deep-thinking question. During the modeling, I like to throw in a deep-thinking question that is completely irrelevant to the text; e.g., if the paragraph is about aboriginal totem pole carving and shows a photograph of the carver, I might point to his T-shirt and ask: "I wonder how much that T-shirt cost?" Some laughter often results. However, it is an important time to stop and reflect on the purpose of asking questions. "Why is that question funny?" (because it has nothing to do with the information in the text) "Why do we ask questions?" (to help us understand the text better) Remind students that when they ask questions about the text, they should make sure their questions are connected to the topic and will help them better understand the information.
- Guide the student to answer with "I think…" or "Maybe…" and then say "That's what I think, what do you think?"
- Give a different answer to the question.
- Repeat the steps, but reverse the roles.
- Extension to Independent Practice: Students find a partner and choose any nonfiction book.
- Partners proceed through the steps of the lesson with one person asking and one person answering.
- Partners reverse roles.

My Wonder Web

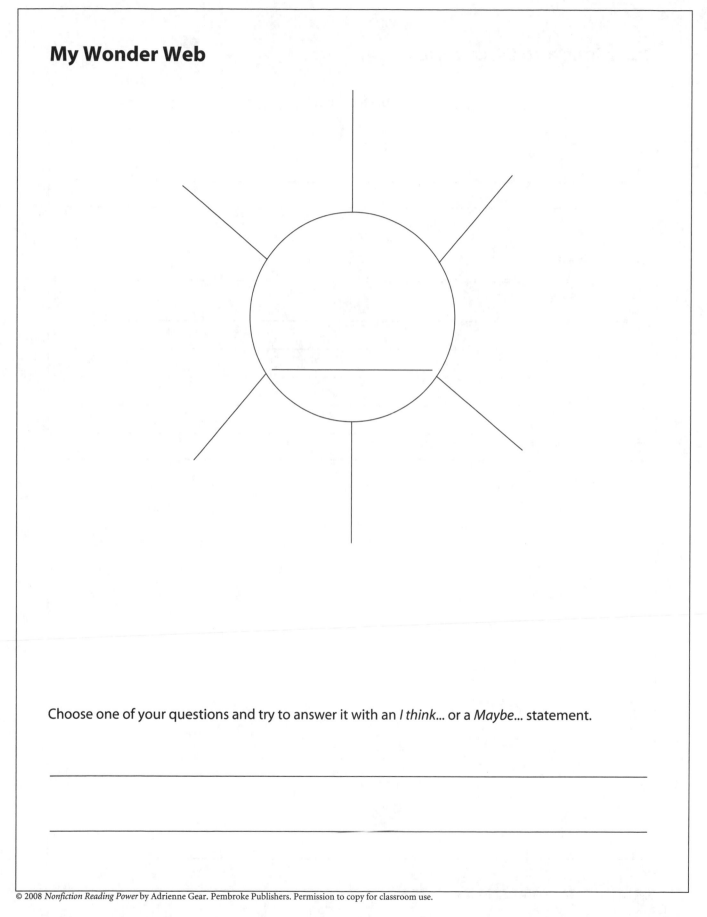

Choose one of your questions and try to answer it with an *I think...* or a *Maybe...* statement.

_____

_____

Questions and Discoveries

_____ 's question about _____ :

_____?

What I discovered:

_____
_____
_____
_____
_____

Introducing the Power to Infer

For this lesson you will need
• the Nonfiction Reading Powers model (page 29)

When I was a student, I found the word "inferring" extremely daunting. It was a concept that I never clearly understood and, apart from the definition of "reading between the lines," it was never really explained to me in a way that made sense. It was something that I was expected to know how to do, yet was never actually taught. For me, inferring was always something "out there"—too complex and too challenging to really figure out. What I realize now is that inferring is really not that complicated. It is, in fact, something that humans do naturally every day: when we see our dog sitting by the back door, when we look at someone's facial expression, when we hear a certain tone in someone's voice. The only problem is, most of us don't realize that what we are doing is inferring. Helping students recognize their own natural ability to infer is the key to later success when we move into text.

• Begin the lesson:

For the past few weeks we've been learning about how active readers ask questions while they read to help them think more deeply about the text. Today we're going to be moving into a new thinking strategy called Inferring.

(Point to *Question/Infer* puzzle piece in head of Nonfiction Reading Powers model.)

Now, some people think inferring is hard to learn, but I'm going to let you in on a little secret: you actually already know how to infer. You just might not know it! Inferring when you read becomes much easier when you understand what it is and how to do it. We're going to start by playing some simple games.

GAME 1: INFERRING FROM AN IMAGE

• Tell students you are going to give them some clues and you want them to try to "infer" what you are feeling.
• Make a pose that depicts a feeling; e.g., surprised, sad, embarrassed. Use your face and body to give clues but don't say anything. Hold the pose for five seconds.
• Ask students to turn and tell their partners what they inferred, and to identify the clues that helped them. Encourage them to use the word "infer":

You might say this: "I inferred that she was surprised. The clues were that her hands went up, her eyes were open wide, her mouth was open and a little smiling."

• Ask students to think about what was missing from your pose.

What are you wondering? (what happened to make you so surprised)

• Have students talk to their partners about a possible cause for the feeling they inferred.
• Have students share some of their "maybes." (Maybe someone you hadn't seen in a long time came into the room. Maybe you just got a new puppy. Maybe someone threw you a surprise party. Maybe you just won a million dollars.)

I model "maybes" that are completely "out there" (e.g., "Maybe an alien just asked you to marry him") to introduce the concept of the "imagination zone," a place frequently visited by certain students. Pointing this out to children, and allowing one "imagination zone" inference first, helps to get the silly comments out of their system so they focus on more appropriate sources for their inferences—background knowledge and experiences.

- Reflect on the "maybes":

  What did you notice about our maybes?" (They were all different) Why were they all different? Where did the maybes come from? (from personal experiences or things we might have seen or wanted)

- Continue the lesson: Model one or two more emotions, or invite students to "strike a pose." With younger students, brainstorm a list of emotions for them to choose from. It's helpful to have them visualize the clues they will be giving the class before they start.

GAME 2: INFERRING FROM WORD CLUES

- Have emotion flash cards prepared ahead of time. Write emotion words on individual flash cards: disappointed, frustrated, worried, etc.
- Ask a volunteer to leave the room.
- Show the class the word, but ask them not to say it.
- Tell them to think of a time when they felt that way.
- Invite the volunteer back into the room. Tell the volunteer to listen to three clues, and then try to infer what the word is.
- Teacher models first:

  I felt that way once when…

- Invite two more students to give clues.
- End the lesson:

  So what we were actually doing in these games was practicing inferring. When you infer, you first look for the clues, then use the clues and your own experiences to try to figure out what's not there. In this case, you looked at the clues to infer what I was feeling, then used your background knowledge and experience to infer what you didn't know—why I was feeling that way.

  When you read, you also infer. And there's a secret to inferring that I wish I had learned a long time ago. Are you ready for the secret? Not all authors tell you everything. And it's not because they lost their pencil or their computer broke or they got tired of writing. Sometimes they leave things out because they want you, the reader, to figure it out for yourself. Inferring is figuring out what the author didn't tell you.

- Prepare an anchor chart to summarize what was learned about inferring.

Inferring: Becoming a Book Detective

Step one
• Look for the clues
Step two
• Ask yourself, "What do I know from the clues?"
• Ask yourself, "What do I NOT know? What is missing?"
Step three
• Use the clues plus your experiences and background knowledge to "fill in" or figure out what is missing.
• Begin your inference with "I think.". or "Maybe.".

Scaffolded Lessons for Inferring

Lesson 1 (Teacher Directed): Observe/Wonder/Infer

For this lesson you will need
- an overhead or large copy of an interesting realistic image: e.g., from *Looking Down* by Steve Jenkins; *Let's Talk About It* photo cards (Mondo Publishing); a newspaper photo or photo from *National Geographic*.
- OWI chart (page 81 or 82) reproduced on large piece of paper

It is a natural progression to move from teaching questioning into inferring, as they're so closely connected. The OWI strategy helps to break down the process of inferring so that it becomes clearer. The students are gradually released from showing the process of their thinking, and will eventually only need to share the inferences.

- Begin the lesson:

  Yesterday we were playing some games to help us learn about inferring. When you infer, you use the clues and your own experiences to fill in what you don't know or is not written. Today we're going to learn a strategy called the *OWI*. OWI stands for Observe, Wonder, Infer, and it will help you understand the steps your brain takes when you are inferring.

- Show image to the students and give them a few moments to look carefully at all the clues in the picture.
- Begin modeling and recording your observations in *Observe* column, using the prompt, "I see…"
- After modeling one or two observations, ask students, "What do you see?" Record their answers in the first column under *Observe*. Young students might have difficulty distinguishing between an observation and an inference. They tend to naturally move straight into the "I think…"s. Be clear that this first part is only for recording what they can *actually see*, not what *they think* is happening or going to happen.
- Now ask students what they are wondering about the picture: "What do you not know but you are wanting to know?" Ask them to share their questions with a partner. Encourage students to ask questions that will deepen their understanding.
- Students share out while you record some of their responses on the chart under *Wonder*.
- If a student asks an irrelevant question—"I wonder if that guy likes cheese pizza?"—respond by reminding students that questions should help them with their understanding.

  I'm wondering how that question will help you with your understanding. You may be curious if the man in this picture likes cheese pizza, but I'm not sure if that information really helps you understand this picture better.

I am often asked what the difference between an inference and a prediction is. In my thinking, a prediction is a level-one inference: while it follows a similar process of filling in what is not yet known, at the end of reading a prediction is either verified or it isn't. With a prediction, as with a quick question, your thinking stops. A true inference, on the other hand, is level-two or deep-thinking, because there is no verification once you have finished reading, and so your thinking keeps going.

- Now tell students to think about the questions they asked and to use the clues in the picture, plus their own experiences and knowledge, to infer. Have them share their inferences with a partner, encouraging them to begin their inference with "I think…" or "Maybe…"
- Students share out, while you record some of their responses on the chart stand under *Infer*.
- If a student offers an obscure or "out there" inference, it is important to address it—once the laughter dies down.

When we make an inference, we are trying to figure out what information is not presented to us. When we do that, we use our thinking, our experiences, and our background knowledge to try to figure it out. It sounds to me as if you used your imagination to infer. Using your imagination to infer would work well if the book we're reading was an imaginary or fantasy story. But when we're reading information that is true, it is important to try to stay away from our imagination zone and focus on our knowledge and our experiences.

- End the lesson:

Today we slowed down our thinking to really understand what happens in our brain when we infer. First, we look and see what information is there. Next, we ask questions. Then we use our own experiences and knowledge to try to "fill in" or infer what's missing. In real life, our brain works much faster, and often our brain sees and wonders so fast that we automatically start to infer when we read.

Lesson 2 (Independent Practice): OWI

- Begin the lesson: Have students choose an image they want to work with and glue it onto their OWI sheet. This lesson can be done individually or with a partner.
- In partners, students first practice the OWI orally, sharing what they observe, their questions, and their inferences stemming from their picture.
- Individually or in pairs, students write some of their observations, questions, and inferences in the appropriate columns on their OWI chart.
- Once the students begin to recognize the difference between an observation and an inference, you can move them from the OWI into the WI (see next lesson).

Lesson 3 (Independent and Guided Practice): Extended OWI

This two-part lesson works well for intermediate students and can be used to teach important events that have shaped and influenced our history. I use images from the National Geographic publication *One Hundred Photographs That Changed the World* (but not all of the images are appropriate for all grade levels).

- Begin the lesson: Divide the class into groups of four or five and give each group one photograph and one Extended OWI chart.
- Students study the photograph and begin to record their observations, questions, and inferences on the upper portion of the chart.
- Groups share out and highlight one or two key questions and inferences
- Continue the lesson (maybe the next day): Pass out the information or text that accompanies the photograph to the groups.
- One student in each group reads aloud the information about the photograph. Students discuss and record their new questions and inferences on the bottom portion of the chart.
- Groups share out their thinking.

Lesson 4 (Independent Practice): Let's Play WI!

As an alternative to the OWI charts used in Lesson 2, the WI chart eliminates the *Observation* column, allowing the students to begin with their questions. This is

For this lesson you will need
- A collection of interesting images or photographs, cut from magazines or newspapers
Each student will need
- OWI Primary chart (page 81) and OWI Intermediate chart (page 82)

For this lesson you will need
- *One Hundred Photographs That Changed The World* or photographs from any news event with accompanying text separated from the photo (students will be given the information later in the lesson): one copy per student
Each student will need
- Extended OWI (page 83)

For this lesson you will need
- cut-out images from *National Geographic* or other magazines; no text attached

Each student will need
- WI chart (page 84)

a two-day activity: students spend the first day focusing on the questions; and then time is spent the next day on selecting one or two deep-thinking questions to stimulate the inferences.

- Begin the lesson: Students choose a photograph that interests them and glue it on their WI sheets.
- Students generate questions about the image and record the questions on their sheets.
- Continue the lesson the next day: Students are asked to read over their questions and choose two that they think are important and can help extend their learning and thinking.
- Remind students to try to choose deep-thinking questions: questions that will help them explore their thinking and help them find meaning in the picture.
- Encourage your students to "show their thinking" when they write their inference.

When recording your inferences today, I want you to really try hard to show me "thinking that keeps going." That means that you don't just answer with a short, quick answer, but you expand your answer to show me your thinking.

- Model the difference between inferences that show that your thinking has stopped and inferences that show your thinking keeps going. Encourage students to "show thinking that keeps going."

Teacher sample on a picture of a man rock climbing.

Question	Inference
How old is he?	I think maybe he's 24. (Thinking that stops)
How old is he?	I think he's 24 because I think you would have to be at least 24 to have enough training to be able to climb that huge mountain. (Thinking that keeps going)

- Students record their inferences on their sheet

WI sample on a picture of a man rock climbing.

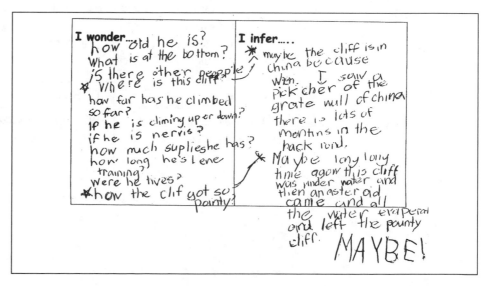

Lesson 5 (Teacher Directed): Moving from Image to Text

For this lesson you will need:
• 1–2 pages from a nonfiction text (can be made into an overhead transparency); e.g., *Ants* by Deborah Hodge (Primary); *Shipwreck on a Sea of Ice* by Matt White (Intermediate)
• Text Questions and Inferences (page 85) enlarged for modeling

As with anything I teach, my goal is for my students to "get it", not just "do it." For the strategy of questioning and inferring, it is of particular importance that I spend time building students' confidence and competence in the actual process of inferring. Beginning with an image that invites the questions, then bridging those questions to inferences, is a way of scaffolding the concepts. It is our goal for students to be asking questions and making inferences with text. It is, therefore, essential that we model how we can take our understanding of questioning and inferring into a text.

• Begin the lesson:

We have been spending the last little while learning and practicing inferring. We've learned that sometimes we need to add our own thinking to things to help us understand information better. Up until now, we've been practicing inferring with pictures. Today we're going to take our understanding of inferring and see what it looks like when we read text. Remember the secret of understanding inferring is that not all authors tell their readers everything. Often they leave things out and it is up to us, the readers, to add our thinking into the text to try to make sense of it.

When using the overhead for a lesson, I like to use paper to cover up sections of the text and only reveal a chunk at a time. This way the students can focus on the information a little at a time.

• Remind the students that when you infer, you first need to look at what the author does tell us, then think about what is missing and what we wonder, then add our "maybes."
• Project overhead transparency sample of nonfiction text and read aloud the first chunk, paragraph, or section.
• Model the process by talking through what you have read.

It says here that…, but I'm wondering….

• Record your fact and question on the chart.

Now I'm going to think about this question and add my maybe.

During this type of guided lesson, I notice that if I model and share my responses with the students first, then my responses become their responses. I recommend allowing time for students to discuss and share their responses first, before sharing your own.

• Have students turn and talk to their partners about their "maybe" to the question they wrote while you record yours on the chart.
• Invite some students to share their thinking. Share your inference.
• Read another chunk of text and repeat, talking through and recording your questions and inferences.

Modeling Inferring: Primary sample on *Ants* by Deborah Hodge

Text Says…	Questions	Inferences
Ants live everywhere in the world, except very cold places.	Why don't ants like very cold places?	"Maybe their bodies or their outer layer would freeze." "Maybe they do not have the ability to regulate their body temperature"

| They dig a home in the soil or make a nest in a tree. | Why do they have two homes? | "Maybe different kinds of ants have different homes."

"Maybe they use the nest for their eggs and the anthill to sleep." |

Text Says…	Questions	Inferences
Twenty-eight joined Shackleton on his expedition to Antarctica	Why would anyone choose to go on an expedition where nobody had ever gone before?	"Maybe they had always wanted to explore places but never had the chance." "Maybe they were bored in their job."
Shackleton's crew lived on an ice floe for over five months	Why would they stay there for so long? What did they do for food?	"Maybe they were waiting to be rescued." "It was winter, so maybe they couldn't travel through the water because it was frozen." "Maybe they ate raw fish and drank melted ice."

Modeling Inferring: Intermediate sample on *Shipwreck and Survival on a Sea of Ice* by Matt White

- There will always be students who ask irrelevant questions. For example, the student who asks: "Did the sailors on Shackleton's ship snore?" It is important to address these questions, guiding these students back to purpose.

  Why are we asking questions? (to help us understand the text better)
    How has your question helped you to understand this information better? (It doesn't.)

  It becomes quickly apparent, if the question is unrelated to the context of the text, that the question was not deepening their understanding.
- End the lesson:

  Today we were taking our understanding of inferring and seeing what it looks like when we read. Breaking down the process helps us to see where our inferences come from. Eventually, we won't need to be writing all this information down. Eventually, our brains will automatically shift into Inferring mode, and we will just add our thinking to the text naturally.

Lesson 6 (Independent Practice): Inferring from Text

For this lesson you will need
- short pieces of nonfiction text or photocopied articles in a range of reading abilities (see Books for Determining Importance on page 90 for suggested resources)

Each student will need
- Questions and Inferences sheet (page 86)

When learning any new strategy, students need lots of practice with texts that are at or below their reading level, so that they can focus on their thinking and gain the confidence they need to move into more complex texts. Introducing the strategy with whole-class instruction, which includes both teacher modeling and guided practice, places every student on an equal playing field. The independent lessons that follow involve all the students working on the same strategy, the only difference being the level of text that they are using.

- Begin the lesson: Students choose, or are assigned, a piece of nonfiction text to read.
- If able, students work independently and complete the sheet.
- Teacher is free to pull small groups who require more instruction and support.

OWI Primary

Name: _____

Glue picture here

Observe	**W**onder	**I**nfer
I see	I wonder…	Maybe…
_____	_____	_____
_____	_____	_____
I see	I wonder…	Maybe…
_____	_____	_____
_____	_____	_____
I see	I wonder…	Maybe…
_____	_____	_____
_____	_____	_____

OWI Intermediate

Name: _____   Title:_____

Glue picture here

Observe	**W**onder	**I**nfer

Extended OWI

Name: _____

Title: _____

What I Observe	What I Wonder	What I Infer
Now I Know...	Now I Wonder...	My Final "Maybes"

WI

Name: _____   Title: _____

Glue picture here

Wonder	**I**nfer

Text Questions and Inferences

Name: _____   Title: _____

Text Says...	Questions	Inferences

Questions and Inferences

Name: _____

Title: _____   Author: _____

My Questions	My Inferences
Something NOT in the text but that you are wondering about. Make sure your question is connected to the meaning.	Answer the questions and add your own thinking to make the text more meaningful. Try to begin your inferences with "I think…" or "Maybe…"

5 The Power to Determine Importance

In our technology-driven world, children are inundated with information—on television, on the Internet, in magazines, and in movie theatres. And while they may be developing strategies to process and sift through the flashy advertisements better than adults, how effectively is this being transferred to the printed page of a real text? In fact, having so much information at their fingertips, children now, more than ever, need to be able to learn to be selective and know where to go to determine what is important. Downloading pages and pages of information for a research project does nothing, if you are not able to determine what's most important.

I made a lot of "connections" to Stephanie Harvey's description of her old university text books, and the pages and pages of highlighted text (Harvey & Goudvis, 2007: 117). Mine look very similar and, although very colorful, clearly reflect my lack of understanding of where to locate important information in a text—how to "get the gist" of a piece. And while the lack of instruction I received in determining main ideas created challenges for me as a reader, it has also motivated me to introduce my students to a variety of strategies so that they can learn to sift through the details, and be able to summarize the main idea. Some of these strategies work better for certain types of readers than others. I believe that it is, therefore, important to introduce readers to a variety of ways of locating main ideas and to allow students to choose the one or ones that work best for them. As with any strategy I teach, the more opportunities the students have to practice the strategies with texts at or below their reading level, the better the chances are that they will apply the strategy when reading independently.

In my search for ways to help students determine importance, I have come across numerous strategies, far too many to include in this book. Being in classrooms and trying these lessons with students has enabled me to find a few that have worked well. These strategies come from different sources and, while I may have adapted and tweaked them, I have made every attempt to credit the original source.

One of my goals was to try to find generic strategies, ones that are not specifically tied to particular text. Most of the lessons here will work with any short piece of text, and it is my recommendation that you use this opportunity to find books that are connected to your social studies and science content areas.

Determining Importance is one of the most important strategies students will learn when reading nonfiction texts. Without the ability to determine what the text is about, there is little or no chance that a student will be able to move forward into interactive and insightful levels of comprehension. Introducing students to different ways to find the main idea, modeling and guiding them through the lessons, and providing opportunities for independent practice with texts at their level will encourage success.

A Note on Text Structure

The concept of text structure, although not new, has been hovering in the back corners of my thinking for the past several years. Until recently, however, I had not considered it to be of particular importance to the reading and under-

As with all the strategies, practicing with texts at or below reading level will promote success.

standing of nonfiction, and it took a backseat to some of the other strategies I considered to be more relevant. It is now becoming more and more evident that to help students determine what is important in nonfiction texts we must give them, at the very least, an introduction to the concept of text structures so that they can begin to recognize the differences in how information is presented.

I was first introduced to the concept of text structures by Tony Stead's *Is That A Fact?* More recently, in their book *Teaching Text Structures: A Key to Nonfiction Reading Success,* Sue Dymock and Tom Nicholson discuss the importance of teaching the different text structures to students in order to enhance their comprehension of nonfiction text. "Readers who understand the many expository text structures, and who use this knowledge as they read, will remember more of the important information in the text" (Dymock & Nicholson 2007: 26). Based on the work of Bonnie Meyer, one of the first researchers to classify nonfiction by different design structures, Dymock and Nicholson's model recommends first introducing the concept of text structures, and then presenting four or five simple structures for nonfiction that students can learn to identify. The text that most students begin to encounter at an elementary school level are descriptive and sequential.

Key Concepts of Text Structure

- Any piece of written text has a text structure.
- A text structure is a way that a piece of writing is organized.
- Fiction (stories, narrative text) has only one text structure: Setting, Characters, Plot; Problem, Solution; Beginning–Middle–End.
- Nonfiction (information, expository text) has several text structures:
    - Descriptive
    - Sequential
    - Compare and Contrast
    - Cause and Effect
    - Problem/Solution
- Paying attention to the structure of a text can help readers locate the important information.

Introducing the Power to Determine Importance

Before launching into a series of strategy lessons, it is important for me to explain to the students the concept: what we are learning and why we need to learn it. Tanny McGregor (2007: 78–80) describes her Purse lesson, in which she pulls out the contents of her purse and lays them on a table in front of her students. Items range from her cell phone and keys to a package of gum and a coupon. She then tells her students that she is going to be jogging around the track after school and doesn't want to take her purse; she wants to carry with her only what is important and leave the rest of the things in her purse. The students have to discuss in partners which items she should take and which she should leave and why. This wonderful and effective concrete example puts a reading strategy into a real-life situation so that students can experience it in its simplest form.

- Begin the lesson:

I'm sure many of you have noticed that, when you read nonfiction books—books on a particular topic or subject, for example—there is often a lot of information presented to you. Some of the information is important; some of it may be interesting details that have been added. Active readers are able to sort out all the information and figure out what really is important. What can be difficult, at times, is trying to figure out what the most important information is and where to find it. The next Reading Power that we are going to be learning is called "Determining Importance."

(Place Determining Importance puzzle piece in head of Nonfiction Reading Powers model.)

I'm going to help you learn different ways to try to figure out and locate the most important parts of nonfiction texts. You will most likely find some ways easier than others, and hopefully you will find one that will work for you.

To get us started, I thought we'd play a little game to get our minds thinking about determining importance. I would like you to imagine that you have been given an opportunity to spend one year alone on a deserted island. If you manage to survive for a year on this island, you will receive a great fortune. You are only allowed to bring with you 15 items. On a scrap piece of paper, I would like you to make a list of the 15 items you would take. Think carefully, now; this island has nothing and you need to survive alone for one year.

- Students write their own lists of 15 items.
- Have students share and compare their lists in partners. Encourage trading or switching list items during sharing time.
- Model and share your own list with the class.
- Tell students that they now need to cut out five items to make a list of ten.
- Model and think aloud as you cut items from your list, justifying why they may not be as important as other items.
- Invite students to cross out five items and then to share their revised lists with a partner.

To survive on an island, I would bring...			
backpack	pajamas	pencil	tarp
water bottle	fishing rod	notebook	sleeping bag

- Repeat the process several more times, until the students are told that they are allowed only three items.
- End the lesson:

Well done, everyone. You all did an excellent job of determining importance—of finding the main items that would help you to survive. But you were also using a very important thinking strategy that active readers use: determining importance. You did it by thinking, by discussing, and by choosing what you felt was most important for your survival. And while everyone's list is not exactly the same, I'm

Convincing your partner that you have made the right choices becomes part of the challenge. The decision-making and deep discussions that occur during this lesson is worth the time it takes.

convinced that none of you ended up with trivial, unimportant items; I know that all the items were very carefully chosen and justified. This is something we need to always keep in mind when we are reading—finding the main idea is not about getting the answer right, it's about thinking through the text to figure out what you want to take away from it. It's about deciding what information you think should be left behind and what information should be "brought to the island."

Books for Determining Importance

Nicola Davies, *Extreme Animals* (I)

Nicola Davies, *Poo* (I)

Stephanie Harvey & Anne Goudvis, *Comprehension Toolkit* (P, I)

Ben Hillman, *How Big is It?* (I)

Ben Hillman, *How Strong is It?* (I)

Evan Moore Publishing, Nonfiction Reading Practice (reproducible units with articles at three different reading levels; available in various grade levels) (P, I)

Evan Moore Publishing, Read and Understand Science (reproducible articles for content area reading practice; available in various grade levels) (P, I)

Cormac O'Brian, *The Daily Disaster: Real Life Stories of 30 Amazing Disasters* (I)

School Specialty Publishing, Extreme Readers series (P)

Louise & Richard Silsbury, World of Plants series (includes *Why Do Plants Have Flowers?*; *Where Do Plants Grow?*) (P)

Diane Swanson, *Up Close: Tails That Talk and Fly* (also *Up Close: Noses That Blow and Poke*) (P)

Diane Swanson, *Animals Eat the Weirdest Things*; *Animals Can Be So Speedy*; *Animals Can Be So Sleepy* (P)

Text on Two Levels series (includes *Energy*; *Geography*; *Solar Power*; *Resources*) (I)

WEBSITES

Sports Illustrated for Kids
http://www.sikids.com/

CBC for Kids
http://www.cbc.ca/kids/

National Geographic for Kids
http://www.nationalgeographic.com/kids/

Time Magazine for Kids
http://timeforkids.org

What in the World?: Current events for Canadian schools
http://www.lesplan.com/main.php

http://www.readinga-z.com

http://www.readingquest.org

http://www.readwritethink.org

http://www.readinglady.org

Scaffolded Lessons for Determining Importance

Lesson 1 (Teacher Directed): THIEVES

This strategy, adapted from the work of S.L. Manz (2002), has been developed for previewing textbooks. I have used it with intermediate students to help them "set the stage" for reading a new chapter in a textbook or for previewing an article or selected portion of a text. It works well for certain types of texts, but not for all.

• Begin the lesson:

We've been talking about determining importance and trying to find the main idea of a piece of text. Sometimes there is a lot of information on a page and not all of it is important. But there are certain places in texts that often have the most important information. If you know where to look for the information, it might help you when you are trying to figure out what information is important. This strategy is called THIEVES—T-H-I-E-V-E-S. I want to spend a little bit of time talking about thieves and what they do. Let's think about thieves who break into a house. Why are they there? (to steal things) Right—they enter the home to steal things. Now let's think about how they go about doing that. Do you think they stand in the hallway and consider where they should look first? Most thieves know what it is they want to steal and, more importantly, where they are going to find it. Where might a thief go to find the "goods" they want to steal? (bedroom, office, living room)

Well today we're going to learn how to be THIEVES when we read. Just like a good thief, a good reader knows where to go in the text to find the "good stuff."

- Proceed through the acronym for THIEVES and explain what each letter stands for. It can be effective to have an overhead transparency of a page and use the strategy directly with a piece of text.

T — Title	
H — Headings	
I — Introduction	
E — Every first sentence	
V — Visuals	
E — Ending	
S — So What?	

- Continue the lesson:

The most important letter is the final letter—*S*—the "So what?" stage. So what do you think the most important ideas of this chapter (or article) are? Turn and talk to your elbow partner.

Having the students make their own THIEVES bookmarks to tuck into their copies of the textbook can be the helpful reminder they need as they read independently. Although it is easy to apply, I believe that had I learned this strategy when I was in high school, I would have saved a significant amount of money on highlighter pens in university.

- End the lesson:
The THIEVES strategy is helpful for trying to determine what is important in a piece of informational text. It's also a way of helping you "get your mind ready" for the article. If you can figure out what the piece is about before you even start to read it, then it makes the reading that much easier. And often you will find that, after reading the main body of the text, you have already found the most important information that you need to know, because you know how to be a THIEF!

Lesson 1 Alternative for Primary Students (Teacher Directed): Take a PEEK

For primary students, a simplified version of the THIEVES strategy can be used when students are previewing simple nonfiction leveled books. This strategy can be used before the students begin to read as a way of setting the stage for reading and for figuring out what the text is about. It is a quick previewing strategy that can be done orally with partners.

For this lesson you will need
- a beginner nonfiction book (a Big Book would work well for this lesson)

- Begin the lesson:

Information books are full of lots of information.

(Hold up book showing a two-page spread)

Sometimes when I look at a page from a nonfiction book, like this one, there is so much information all over the page that I don't know where to start! Sometimes it helps, before I start to read everything, to take a PEEK at what's here so that I can figure out, before I start to read, what things on this page might be important. This quick little activity is called "Take a PEEK." It is a way of just helping me prepare for reading the page.

- Write the word *PEEK* vertically on the board or chart paper.

Pictures
Each heading
Ending
Know

The letter *P* stands for Pictures. Before I read the page, I'm going to look at all the pictures. Looking at the pictures helps to get my brain focused on what the page is about and things that might be important.

The first letter *E* stands for Every Heading. We know that information on a page is sometimes organized into sections. Reading the titles and headings on the page helps get my brain focused on the information.

The second letter *E* stands for Ending. Sometimes the end of a book or a chapter retells important facts. Reading the ending first can help to focus my brain on what information might be important.

The last letter, *K*, stands for Know. What do I know about this book (page)? What is this book (page) about? Now remember, we haven't read it all yet, but sometimes if we can think about what we know from our little "peek," then it helps us focus our brains on what is important.

P — Pictures
E — Each heading
E — Ending
K — Know now? (What do I now know that might be important in this book?)

- Continue the lesson:

Now let's try to "Take a PEEK" with this book. Who can remember what *P* stands for? Right—so I'm going to look at all the pictures and think about what I see.

(Discuss the photos.)

Who can remember what *E* stands for? Right—now I'm going to read all the headings on the page.

Now I'm going to look at the ending to see if there is important information here.

Now I'm going to ask myself what I now know about this book. Remember, I haven't read it all yet, but I've taken a peek.

Turn to your partner and tell them what you now know.

- Model what you know about the page.
- End the lesson:

"Take a PEEK" is something that readers can do before they start to read an information book. It only takes a few minutes, but it is a good way of focusing our brains on what we are going to read and helps us to figure out what information is important.

- Independent Practice: Students can choose their own books and practice "Take a PEEK" independently or with partners.

Lesson 2 (Teacher Directed/Guided Practice): Turning It into a Question

This simple, effective strategy takes no prep but works well to help guide readers into locating important key pieces of text. It takes the simple principal of turning each title and heading into a question and then reading to find the answer. Often the title or heading will point readers in the right direction.

- Begin the lesson:

Today I'm going to show you a quick strategy that can help you locate the main idea from a piece of text. It combines two strategies we have already learned— Zooming-In on text features and asking Questions. As we have learned, information on a page is often organized into sections with headings.

(Point to headings on transparency)

As you can see here, this article has a title and several headings. We are going to use these headings to help focus our reading and to determine the main points of this article.

First, I'm going to copy the title onto this chart. The title of this article is *A Mammal, Not a Fish.*

(Copy into *Heading* column)

Now in this column I'm going to turn that heading into a question. What question could I write?

- Model turning the heading into a question and record it in the *Question* column (see example on page 94).
- Record the second heading.
- Invite the students to participate by sharing a possible question with a partner.
- Invite students to provide the questions and record them on the chart. Continue guiding and modeling.
- Continue the lesson:

Now I'm going to read this article to try to find the answers to these questions. I'll use these questions to guide me to determining the main ideas of this article. The first question I have written here is "What is a mammal?" I'm going to read this section to try to find the answer to this question.

- Read aloud the section and model answering and recording on the chart.
- Continue to read each section, reminding students that they are reading to try to answer the question.
- After modeling one or two examples, invite the students to participate to complete the chart.

For this lesson you will need
- overhead transparency of a nonfiction text for modeling: e.g., *Whales and Dolphins* by Caroline Bingham

Look for a page that includes a title and several headings or subheadings.

- End the lesson:

  Using the headings to help guide our reading is a way for us to find the important information in a text. Turning those headings into questions and answering the questions helps us focus on the important facts rather than the details.

Sample on *Whales and Dolphins* by Caroline Bingham, pages 4–5.

Title or Heading	Turn it Into a Question	Read to answer the question
A Mammal, Not a Fish	What is a mammal?	*- warm blooded*
	Why are they not fish?	*- lungs not gills*
		- come to surface to breathe
Breathe In	How do mammals breathe?	*- draw air through blowhole not mouth*
Blubber for Warmth	How does blubber keep them warm?	
Helping Hair	How does hair help?	

Lesson 3 (Independent Practice): Turn It into a Question!

For this lesson each student will need:
• a nonfiction book
• Turn It Into a Question sheet (page 102)

- Begin the lesson: Students may work individually or in pairs.
- Have students choose their own nonfiction book.
- Have them search for a page or two-page spread that has several headings and titles.
- Students record headings, form questions, and read to answer.

Lesson 4 (Teacher Directed): Introducing Nonfiction Text Structures

As with everything I teach, I believe that awareness of the concept is the key to understanding and application. This lesson introduces students to the concept of text structure and the five different structures most commonly used in informational texts.

For this lesson you will need
• chart paper or SMART board for modeling

- Begin the lesson:

  We are learning different ways to determine what is most important in a piece of informational text. Today we are going to take a look at text structure, or the way a piece of text is designed. Knowing how text is designed or structured can help you figure out what is most important.

  Text structure is the way an author organizes and puts together ideas. Every piece of text has a structure to it, or an "architectural design." Does anyone know what an architect does? (designs buildings) Let's compare an architect to an author for a moment. Let's say that an architect is designing a house. A house has a basic structure to it—a roof, walls, doors, windows. Each house may look different, but inside the structure is the same. So an architect begins with the basic structure of a house and then adds details to make the house unique. If an architect is designing a skyscraper, the structure will be very different from that of a house—more floors, more windows, elevators, stairways. Again, the architect begins with the basic structure and then adds the details. A writer does something very similar, but instead of designing buildings like an architect does, a writer designs text. Let's say a writer was going to write a story. A story has its own structure or framework—setting, characters, plot; problem, solution. The writer begins with this structure for writing a story, then adds details to make the story unique. If a writer is going to write an informational piece about penguins, he or she would use a different structure from that used for writing a story. The writer would begin with the basic structure for describing something, and then add specific details about the penguin.

Everything we read has a structure to it. There are different structures for different types of texts. Knowing what the structure is can really help you understand the text better.

Fiction writing, or stories, have only one structure: setting, characters, plot; problem, solution. All stories have the same structure, and the added details make each story different. Nonfiction, or writing that is true or presents information, has several different text structures. Knowing the different nonfiction text structures can help you become a better reader and can also help you when you are writing.

The first text structure is called *Description*. This is one of the most common text structures for the nonfiction that we read in school. This structure organizes facts that describe specific places, persons, things, or events. If you are reading a book about birds, about a dinosaur, a planet, a country—these would all be descriptive. Descriptive text structure, or the architectural design that we sometimes use for description, is a *web*.

(Draw a web on the chart paper or SMART board.)

The topic is in the middle, and circles around it contain the details about the topic. If you are reading a description, it's easy to figure out the main ideas by using a web like this and filling in the important ideas.

The second text structure is called *Sequential* structure. This is a common nonfiction text structure for anything that is written in steps or in order of appearance; for example, if you are reading about an event in history, the instructions to a game, a recipe, or something that appears in order, like planets in the solar system. The visual that can help us read sequential texts looks like this.

(Draw on chart paper or SMART board.)

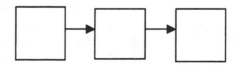

Or sometimes, the boxes might be going up and down like this.

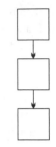

If you are reading anything that outlines something in order, you can put each event into one of these boxes and it will help you figure out the main idea of the text.

- Continue the lesson: Introduce the different text structures: Compare and Contrast, Cause and Effect, Problem/Solution. Draw the visual framework for each (see Text Structure Grid on pages 103–104).
- End the lesson:

Today we've been learning about text structures, the frame that a writer uses to organize ideas, just like the frame an architect uses to design a house. How can knowing the text structure help you with your understanding? (helps you locate important information; helps with note-taking; helps organize your thinking)

- Extend the lesson: After the students have been introduced to text structures, it is important that they be given opportunities to practice determining the text structure of different pieces of text. This could be done very simply in the form of a game:

NAME THAT TEXT STRUCTURE

- Read or display different articles or texts; making overhead transparencies works well. Give students one minute to either read or listen while you read. The first person to correctly determine the text structure wins a point for his/her team or row.

- Another extension would be to model and guide the students how to use the specific visual to record the main ideas from the text, once the text structure has been determined; this helps to structure note-taking. These visuals can also be used for planning a piece of writing.

Lesson 5 (Teacher Directed/Guided Practice): Key Words

This strategy, adapted from Jan Wells and Janine Reid (2004: 64–65) offers a strategy for students to learn to select "key words" from a piece of text, and use them to summarize the main idea.

- Begin the lesson:

We've been working on ways that readers can locate and find the main idea in a nonfiction text. Today we're going to be learning about key words. A key word is a word that contains an important idea from the text. In any piece of text, there are

For this lesson you will need:
- overhead transparency of a one-page article or nonfiction piece (see sample "At the Front of the Cave" on page 105)
- sticky notes to cover up portions of the text
Students will need
- paper for writing a list of key words
- form for Key Words 1 (page 106) or Key Words 2 (page 107)

many words; some words are important and some are less important. Finding important key words can really help us separate what is important from the details that may not be as important.

- Project overhead transparency article "At the Front of the Cave" (or any other single-page article), using sticky notes to cover the entire text except for the title.
- Show title and ask students to select one word, from the six words in the title, that they think is the key word in the title.
- Students share their choice with a partner and explain why they chose the word.
- Remove the sticky notes from the headings, keeping the rest of the article covered.
- Ask the students to talk to a partner about what they think the article will be about. Have some students share out their ideas.
- Repeat the process by removing the sticky notes from visuals, photos, and captions while keeping the main body of the text covered. Students discuss in partners their growing knowledge about what the piece is probably about.
- Decide as a group what the article is most likely going to be about (i.e., rock hyraxes). Ask students to write the topic on the top of their paper. Explain that they will be making a list of key words about the topic.
- Remove the sticky notes from the first paragraph or chunk of text and ask students to read the exposed text carefully. You may also read it aloud.
- Ask students to select three key words they think are the most important words. Have them write those words in a list under the topic on their paper.
- Students share and compare their list with a partner, discussing their choices and the reason for them.
- After the students share, share your own choices with them.
- Continue the lesson:

Can anyone tell me how you made your choices? What helped you decide on your key words?

- As you guide them to articulate how best to look for a key word, write the points on chart paper to create an anchor chart on key words.

The Search for Key Words

Look for…

- Words connected to the topic

- Words that are repeated in the title, headings, or text

- Words that help you visualize

- One word that helps you remember an important idea

- Continue the lesson: Remove sticky notes from each paragraph or chunk, then have students add key words to their list (usually two words per paragraph, but this will vary depending on the length of text).
- Students share and compare their lists, removing or changing words as they go.

For this lesson I purposely choose three words *not* connected to the text or topic. I justify my choices and then have the students tell me why they think that they were not appropriate choices. By "playing dumb" and having the students tell me how to locate key words, they will take more ownership of the strategy. Had I begun the lesson telling them how to find key words, it would not have been as effective.

- End the lesson: Once the list is finalized, have students copy the words from their lists onto a Key Words form. Using the words on their list, students write a short summary on their Key Words form. A labeled picture can also be included.
- Extend the lesson: Using the next lesson, Sum It Up, as a follow-up helps students learn to summarize more effectively.

In this sample, the Grade 3 student has used all key words, but needs support in combining sentences. Using two key words in one sentence helps create a more fluent paragraph and eliminates choppy "robot talk."

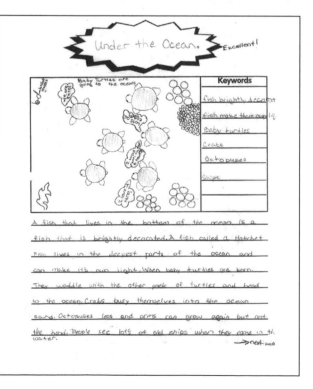

This student's summary ended up longer than the text itself—not an uncommon occurrence, as students often insert information from their background knowledge in their summary. Using a strategy such as Sum It Up (page 99) helps cut down on the extra information.

Lesson 6 (Teacher Directed): Sum It Up

For this lesson you will need
• the list of Key Words from Lesson 5: Key Words (page 96)
• chart paper or SMART board to model

Writing a summary can be challenging for many of us. It's hard to know how much information to include and how much to leave out. Students often have difficulty writing a summary, as their background knowledge tends to filter its way through—this results in a *War and Peace* version of the text, rather than the *Coles Notes* version. I discovered through ReadingQuest.org this fun, engaging strategy that ties the concept of spending money to writing a summary. Students also learn how to combine several key ideas into one sentence.

• Begin the lesson:

We've been looking at ways of locating important information in texts. It's important that you also know how to present that information in a few short sentences. When you take a lot of information and condense it into something smaller, it's called summarizing. The smaller condensed version is called a summary. A good summary includes only the important information from a text and leaves out a lot of the details. Today, I'm going to show you a fun way to write a summary using a strategy called Sum It Up. The "Sum" stands for summary, but it also stands for adding.

Here is a list of key words that I chose from the piece we read yesterday.

Rock Hyraxes	
cave	sun-seeker
shelter	herbivore
enemies	family
mammals	weather

Using these key words, I'm going to write a summary. But there's a trick to this: each word is worth ten cents. The challenge is to try to write a summary paragraph for $2.00 or less, using all the words on my list. Apart from the topic—Rock Hyraxes—I have eight words on my list, which means that all together, they are worth 80 cents. I have $1.20 beyond that to spend, so I had better be very careful in choosing other words. Oh—and since I'm feeling generous today, the topic word is FREE! So I don't need to count the words "rock hyrax" when they appear together. When you play Sum It Up, you also need to think about combining a lot of your key words into one or two sentences.

• Model with your list how several words can be linked together into one sentence.

So here's my start:

Rock hyraxes are small mammals that use caves as shelter from weather and enemies.

So far, I have written 14 words, and two don't count, so I've spent $1.20. That means I have 80 more cents to spend—or eight more words to write. Since I've used four words from my list, four of the remaining eight words need to be words from my list. I still have some important information that I need to include, so I'll need to add another sentence. I may need to rework this first sentence after I write the other one.

Now see what you can do with your list.

- Allow students time to write their summaries.
- Students share with a partner, helping each other if they have "spent" too much.
- Invite some students to read their summaries aloud.
- End the lesson:

Today we learned an easy way to write a summary paragraph. It's not always going to be easy to summarize for $2.00 or less, but it's something to keep in mind when you are asked to write the main ideas from a piece of text. Summaries should include the most important ideas and not have a lot of extra details added.

Lesson 7 (Teacher Directed/Guided Practice): Listen, Sketch, Label, Summarize

Although visualizing is not a specific strategy I focus on for nonfiction reading, because of the many visuals included in most nonfiction texts, it is a strategy that can be extremely effective for determining importance. Creating mental images of key ideas helps visual learners to filter out details and remember the important points. This strategy, adapted from the work of Faye Brownlie, has been proven most effective in many classrooms.

For this lesson you will need
- a one-page nonfiction article for reading aloud, appropriate to grade level

Students will need
- Listen, Sketch, Label, Summarize (page 108) or Draw It/Recall It! (page 109)

- Begin the lesson:

Sometimes, when I'm reading nonfiction, I find that visualizing while I read helps me to remember what's important. Details are often hard to visualize, so visualizing really helps readers to leave out details and focus on the main points. Today we're going to be practicing the strategy of visualizing.

- Read aloud the article from beginning to end and ask students to try to visualize, or create mental images, while they listen.
- Read through the article a second time, pausing between paragraphs or chunks of text to allow students to record a quick sketch that will help them remember that part of the text.
- Ask students to label their sketch with a few key words (not sentences).
- Continue to read the article, pausing between paragraphs for students to add to their sketch.
- Students get together with a partner and "point and talk" through their sketches, retelling what they remember from the article.
- Students use their sketches and key words to write on the bottom of their worksheets a summary of the important points (Using the Sum It Up lesson works well here. See page 99.)
- End the lesson:

Often, I will collect the sketches and continue the lesson the next day. It is amazing how much of the article the students remember from their sketches, even after a day has passed—evidence that the visual memory is a powerful one.

How many of you noticed that visualizing helped you sort out the main idea from all the details? Making mental pictures of information is a great way of remembering what's important. I sometimes keep sketch paper beside me when I am reading information. Sketching the key ideas helps me understand what I'm reading and also helps me better remember it.

Text used for this lesson came from "The Case Against Soda" in *Comprehension Toolkit* by Stephanie Harvey and Anne Goudvis (2005: 100).

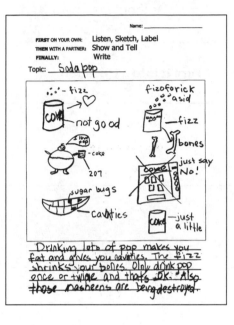

Turn It into a Question

Name: _____   Date: _____

Title of Book: _____   Author: _____

Title or Heading	Turn It into a Question	Read to Answer the Question

Text Structure Grid

Text Structure	What Is It?	Visual	Questions to Ask	Signal Words	Examples
Descriptive	Organizes facts that describe specific places, persons, things; facts being described are not time or order specific		• What is being described? • What are the most important characteristics or attributes of the thing being described? • What does it look like (act like, smell like, feel like, sound like)? • Why is the description important?	Action words (*explode, unfold, nibbles*) Linking verbs (*is, are, belong to*) Present tense (*are, exit, grow*) Factual descriptions, not imaginative language	Report on animal, insect, habitat, clouds, a country, a planet, etc.
Sequential or Chronological	Organizes events in order of their appearance; events are time and/or sequentially specific.		• What sequence of events is described? • What happened first, next, etc.? • What are the main incidents? • How is the pattern revealed?	*before* *during* *after* *finally* *immediately* *initially* *following* *as soon as* *later* *next* *meanwhile* *now* *soon* *then* *until* *today*	• Describe the sequence of events in history • Recount the order of events in a newspaper report • Instructions on how to do or make something • Recount key events in a person's life (biography) • Describe life cycle of a plant or animal

Text Structure Grid, continued

Structure	Description	Graphic	Questions	Signal Words	Topics
Compare and Contrast	Organizes information according to similarities and differences.		• What is being compared? • How are they alike? • How are they different? • What conclusion is drawn? • How is the pattern shown?	*although* *both* *but* *in common* *as well as* *compared to* *either* *as opposed to* *still* *yet*	Compare similarities and differences between • two or more countries • two or more habitats • two or more animals or insects • two or more religions
Problem and Solution	Provides information about a problem and suggests alternatives for solution.		What is the problem? • What has caused this problem? • What are the possible ways to solve the problem?	*A problem is* *A solution is* *The problem is solved by* *propose* *conclude* *The evidence is* *The reason for* *One reason is* *The issues are*	• Problem: litter on the school ground • Problem: my friend is leaving me out at recess • Problem : inevitable shortage of water on the planet • Problem: global warming
Cause and Effect	Tells how one or more event(s) causes another event(s) to follow as a result.		What is the event being described? • What factors contributed to this event? • What are the consequences or effects which may result from this?	*as a result* *because* *This led to* *nevertheless* *If… then* *so that* *thus* *accordingly* *so* *consequently*	• Effects of poor eating habits on health • Effects of pollution and gas emission on global warming • Effects of the pine beetle on wildlife and industry

At the Front of the Cave

Rock Hyraxes

The entrance of the cave is one place where animals seek shelter from their enemies and the weather. The *rock hyraxes* of Africa, Arabia and Asia use caves or crevasses in rocks and boulders as places to hide.

Hyraxes are mammals that look like furry guinea pigs, only slightly larger. Because hyraxes are defenceless creatures, they depend on the safety of their shelter for survival.

Families of rock hyraxes sun themselves for several hours in the morning before beginning their search for food. They eat mainly berries and plants, and can go for long periods of time without water.

Eagles, large cats and pythons are among the enemies of the rock hyrax. Whenever danger is near, rock hyraxes will escape into caves for safety.

Adapted from *Cave Dwellers* (2004: 5–6)

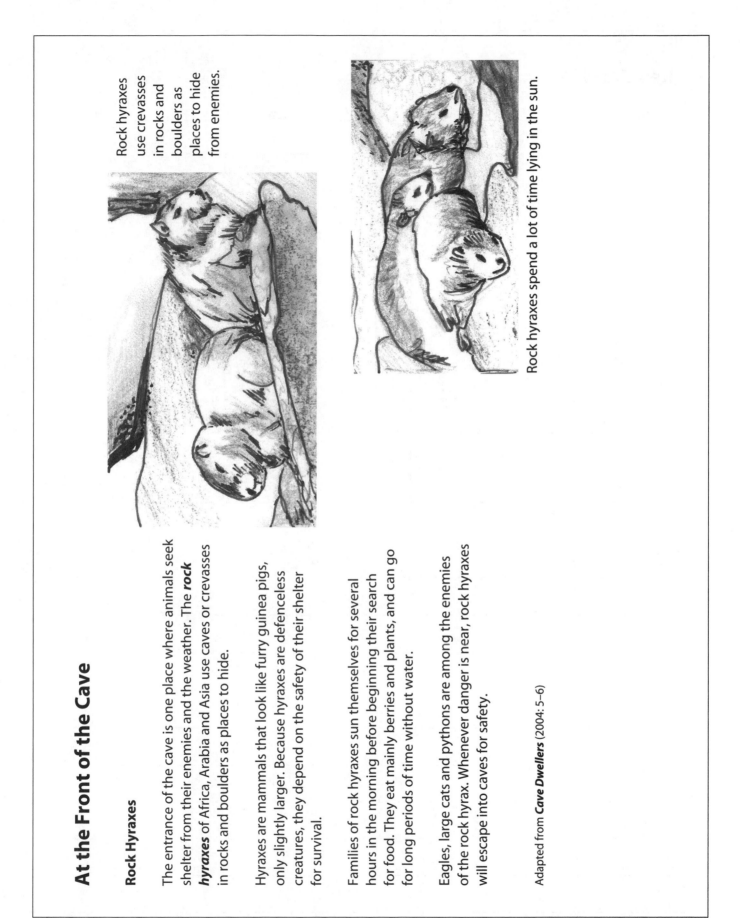

Rock hyraxes use crevasses in rocks and boulders as places to hide from enemies.

Rock hyraxes spend a lot of time lying in the sun.

Key Words 1

Name: _____   Date: _____

<table>
<tr><td></td></tr>
</table>

<table>
<tr><td></td></tr>
<tr><td></td></tr>
<tr><td></td></tr>
<tr><td></td></tr>
<tr><td></td></tr>
<tr><td></td></tr>
<tr><td></td></tr>
<tr><td></td></tr>
</table>

_____

_____

_____

_____

_____

_____

_____

Key Words 2

Name: _____ Date: _____

Topic:_____

Section #1	Section #2	Section #3

Summary:

_____

_____

_____

_____

_____

_____

_____

_____

_____

_____

Listen, Sketch, Label, Summarize

Name: _____   Date: _____

FIRST, ON YOUR OWN: Listen, Sketch, Label
THEN, WITH A PARTNER: Point and Talk
FINALLY, ON YOUR OWN: Write

Topic: _____

_____

_____

_____

_____

_____

Draw It/Recall It!

Name: _____   Date: _____

Text: _____

Draw an image that represents a main idea from your reading.	Write three facts about the main idea you have drawn.
	1. _____ 2. _____ 3. _____
	1. _____ 2. _____ 3. _____
	1. _____ 2. _____ 3. _____
	1. _____ 2. _____ 3. _____

Adapted from *Moving Up With Literacy Place* (2008:102)

6 The Power to Connect

Go to where you know—the place you know best: the deep contours of your head and your heart where memories, experiences, and knowledge lie. This is the place where you will find everything you need to make sense of the world. Depend on it. It is always with you, growing and changing as you live and breathe and think and feel and learn.

"Connecting what readers know to new information is the core of learning and understanding."—Stephanie Harvey (2007: 17)

"The world is made up of stories, not of atoms."—Muriel Rukeyser

I have always believed that the heart of comprehension lies in your understanding and ability to make connections. Connecting is the foundation upon which all other strategies are built. When you go to your own place of knowing—your inner thoughts, ideas, memories, knowledge, and emotion—comprehension, in its truest form, can occur.

In the 1980s, cognitive psychologists devised schema theory to explain how our previous experiences, knowledge, emotions, and understanding affect what and how we learn (Anderson & Pearson, 1994). Having awareness that this place of knowing is the source for understanding is equally as important as the process itself. Building a metacognitive awareness in your students is central for success. Many professionals in the field of comprehension, including Stephanie Harvey and Anne Goudvis, refer to this "place of knowing" as your *schema*. A schema is the part of your brain that contains your ideas, experiences, and knowledge. Everyone's schema is different because everyone's life is different. Many teachers use this reference to schema successfully when teaching their students to make connections. I use a slightly different approach, although the concept is the same. When teaching students to make connections, I refer to schema as "life story":

> Your life is a story. It's just not written down on paper. When you read a story, see if you can "find the chapter" in your own life story that will help you understand the story that you are reading better.

I use this same analogy with my own children, Spencer and Oliver. Whenever our family sets out to do something, or go somewhere, I will often say, "I'm so excited! I get to add another chapter to my life story!" Once, after an exceptionally poor inning of pitching during a baseball game, Spencer came off the field and said, "Mum, don't say anything. It was just a really bad chapter." My younger son, Oliver, had a slightly different approach one day on the way to his first-ever lacrosse game. I asked him if he was nervous and he replied, "Well, I'm not really nervous. I'm just trying to find my lacrosse chapter, but there isn't one!"

One of the questions I am frequently asked by teachers is, "How can I help my students go deeper?" Their students are asking the questions and making the connections, but lack the depth of understanding that we all hope they might reach. I try to help move the students from the surface of understanding to a deeper level by identifying and modeling the difference between quick-thinking and deep-thinking connections. Just as there are quick and deep-thinking questions, so too are there quick and deep-thinking connections. Using the same language to distinguish between effective and less-effective thinking helps reinforce to students that there are levels of understanding to strive for. It is no longer enough for students to be going through the motions of making connections or asking questions; they must demonstrate a deeper layer to their thinking.

Lack of background knowledge and experiences can have a huge impact on students' learning and understanding. I have heard it expressed on more than one occasion that poor reading scores are a direct result of students' lack of background knowledge, that students can't make connections because they have no experiences. The fact that our students may be lacking in background knowledge and experiences should not be held against them—isn't that what they are in school for? To learn and build knowledge is the purpose of education.

Bringing It Back to the Book

Over the past several years, I have had the privilege of seeing Reading Power evolve in different classrooms. I have visited classrooms where the language of thinking was being integrated into all aspects of reading and learning. I have witnessed children moving from making those quick, surface connections ("That reminds me of my dog! My dog has brown fur too!") to deep-thinking connections: "That reminds me of the feeling I had when my dog didn't come home and I felt so worried that she was lost for good."

In one Grade 2/3 classroom, the teacher and I were working together on helping the children make deep-thinking connections. She was so proud of the students' progress and I sat and listened to many deep-thinking connections that day. After the students had shared all of their deep-thinking connections and the lesson ended, the teacher looked at me proudly and said, "Aren't they doing well?" I felt a little sick in my stomach. Although the children were going deeper with their connections, a monumentally important factor was being left out.

The purpose of making connections is not to talk about ourselves. The purpose of making connections is to help the reader understand the story or text better. So, while finding those connections is the first step, the next step is to be able to articulate how that connection has helped you to better understand *this story*. Unfortunately, those students never got there: they shared their stories, but didn't bring their connections back to the story they were reading. At that moment I knew that we had been missing the most essential part of the power to Connect—bringing it back.

The next week, I returned to the classroom, bringing with me a plastic baby bib. On the bib, I have written the letters *BIBB* — Bring It Back to the Book. I addressed the class:

> Last week, when I was visiting, I heard all of you make some amazing connections to the book your teacher read. But today I want to teach you an important thing about connecting that comes after you find your connection.

I then proceeded to model that the reason we make connections is not to talk about ourselves, but instead to help us understand the story we are reading better. The story I read was *Nana Upstairs, Nana Downstairs* by Tomie de Paola, about a boy who lives in a house with one grandma living upstairs and one grandma living downstairs. In the story, one of the grandmas dies. It is a story of grieving and loss and gratitude for a life lived.

This story reminds me of when my Grannie got very sick. Grannie lived with us when I was little, and I remember coming home from school one day and my mum telling me that Grannie had fallen and was in the hospital. I remember the feeling of being so scared and so worried that Grannie was not going to come home again.

(*I tied on my plastic bib. The children laughed, of course.*)

This is my BIBB. BIBB stands for Bring it Back to the Book. When we make connections, it is important to remember how the connection helps you understand the story better by bringing the connection back to the story. This connection to my Grannie helped me to understand the story better, because now I know how the little boy in this story felt being sad about his grandma. I know that because I had the same feeling when my Grannie got sick.

Just as all new things we teach, the BIBB needs to be modeled and practiced with students in order for them to get it. The plastic bib is a way of reminding students the purpose of connecting. Once they have practiced BIBB with connecting, it can be applied to the other reading powers.

A plastic bib may seem a little young for intermediate classes. One teacher suggested that a sports bib (pinny) be used for this lesson, rather than the baby bib.

Introducing the Power to Connect

As with any of the Reading Power strategies, beginning with a lesson on the concept of the strategy is very important. Most students can quickly learn to say "that reminds me of" when reading a piece of text, but how often are they just saying the words, rather than really going deeper into their understanding? Spending time on the concept of connecting—why we connect, where we go to find our connections, how those connections help us make sense of text—is a valuable introduction to this power.

For this lesson you will need
• one book
• the Nonfiction Reading Powers model (page 29)

• Begin the lesson:
   Today we're going to start looking at a new Nonfiction Reading Power—the power to make connections to text.

   (Place Connect puzzle piece in the head of the Nonfiction Reading Powers model.)

   Many of you have already learned how to make connections when you are reading fiction and stories. But I want to spend a little time today thinking about what it really means to make connections: where our connections come from and why we make connections.
   I'd like everyone to make a circle with your finger and your thumb on one hand. Now make another circle with your finger and your thumb on the other hand. On the count of three, I'd like everyone to connect their circles together, any way you like. Try not to look at your neighbor when you are doing this. Think for a minute now how you might connect your circles. Ready? One, two three… connect your circles.

• Have students share their finger connections with their partner.

- Ask volunteers to hold up their finger connections and explain how they connected their circles.

What did you notice about what happened when we all connected our circles? (There were differences.) Even though we were all doing the same thing, many of us found a different way to connect our circles.

- Ask for words that mean the same as connect: *joining, linking, putting together, merging.*
- Remind students that there is no one way to make a connection. Finding the connection that helps you make sense of what you are reading is what is important.
- Move the circle demonstration into reading by holding up the book.

Today we are talking about connecting to books. So here's a book and I'm going to pretend that one of my circles is the book. Show me—where is the other circle going to go? Show me on your body.

(Students put their finger circles on their foreheads, indicating that it is inside the brain where connections are found.)

I see that you are pointing to your head… could you tell me a little more about that. What's inside your head? (memories, experiences, imagination, thoughts, ideas, information, knowledge)

So my brain is amazing. What you are telling me is that it basically holds my entire life inside it—and it's actually not that big.

Let's pretend for a moment that our brains don't have the ability to store memories, and that we have to write everything down on paper. Every experience we have would "add another chapter" to our life story, and our entire life written down would make up a book. Think about how big your book might be; show me with your hands. How big would mine be? How big would your grandmother or grandfather's book be? How big would a Kindergarten kid's be? Someone in Grade 7? A brand new baby has a very small book. But the great thing about a brand new baby's life story—and everyone's life story—is that it just keeps getting bigger. Everything you do and everything you learn adds to your life story. Is every chapter in your life story happy? No, I would think that everyone has some sad chapters and some exciting chapters and some adventure chapters. Is everyone's life story the same? Of course not, because we are all different and we have different lives and different life stories.

But the good news is, we don't have to write our lives on paper, because our amazing brains hold all our stories and knowledge inside. And this is the place we go to find all our connections. If you can find a connection to something that you already have inside your head, then it helps you make sense of what you are reading.

Some students will already be familiar with making connections. If so, your introduction can be shortened. However, reminding students about where our connections come from helps to reinforce the concept and allows everyone to reach even ground.

Books for Connecting

P = primary
I = intermediate

There are some subject areas that are particularly suited to making connections, depending on the grade you teach. Integrating this strategy into your content teaching is highly recommended. (See List of Books by Subject on pages 33–44.)

CELEBRATING DIVERSITY

Anne Claybourne, *Usborne Book of Peoples of the World* (I)

Beatrice Hollyer, *Wake Up World! A Day in the Life of Children Around the World* (I)

Bobbie Kalman, *Canada From A–Z* (I)

FAMILY/COMMUNITY

Paulette Bourgeois, In My Neighbourhood series (P)

Bobbie Kalman, *What is a Community A–Z* (P)

Barbara Kerley, *You and Me Together: Moms, Dads and Kids Around the World* (P)

Joan Sweeny, *Me and My Family Tree* (P)

HUMAN BODY

Aliki, *My Five Senses* (P)

Brigid Avison, *I Wonder Why I Blink: And other Questions About My Body* (I)

Bobbie Kalman, *I Am A Living Thing* (P)

Diane Swanson and Trudee Romanek, *Mysterious You* (I)

Joan Sweeny, *Me and My Amazing Body* (P)

SEASONS

Grace Lin, *Our Seasons* (P)

Claire Llewellyn, *Paint a Sun in the Sky: A First Look at Seasons* (P)

Anne Rockwell, *Four Seasons Make a Year* (P)

WEATHER

David Suzuki, *Looking At Weather* (I)

Neil Waldman, *Snowflake: A Water Cycle Story* (I)

Valerie Wyatt, *Weather FAQ's (Frequently Asked Questions)* (I)

Scaffolded Lessons for Connecting

Lesson 1 (Teacher Modeling): Knew–New Connections

For this lesson you will need
• a blank file folder
• Knew–New Connections (page 120) enlarged for modeling
• a short nonfiction article or section of book: e.g., "Tarantulas" from *Unusual Spiders* in the Take Two series

One of the main differences between connections to fiction and connections to nonfiction lies with the source, where the connections come from. When connecting to fiction, readers usually use connections to personal experiences—find the right chapter in their life stories—to help them make meaning. With nonfiction texts, personal connections are evident, but often are not as prominent. It is difficult to make personal experience connections to something we have not experienced. We can, however, make connections, because we may have read other books, seen videos, looked at photographs, etc. about the topic. We can make connections to background knowledge. Rather than finding a chapter in a life story, it is like finding the right file folder full of articles, images, clippings, etc. Connecting to what is known helps to ground the reader and open him or her up for learning new content, moving from the "knew" to the "new."

Familiar territory paves the way to unfamiliar text.

• Begin the lesson:

Today, readers, we are going to be talking about making connections. Who can tell me what connecting to texts is? Many of you have learned about making connections to stories or to fiction. Making connections with nonfiction or information texts can be a little different from connecting to fiction. When we connect to fiction, we often find connections to our own personal experiences. This is not as easy to do when we are reading nonfiction, because often we're reading about things that we may not have actually experienced; for example, if I'm reading about Mars and I've never been to Mars before. However, sometimes when we read information, we make connections to things that we already know, information in the book that we have heard before. We call this making connections to background knowledge. I like to think of my background knowledge as a file folder of facts that I have stored in my brain.

(Hold up file folder.)

We talk about your brain holding the "chapters" of your life story; your brain also holds "file folders" filled with information that you already know. The facts that we already have in our file folder help us learn more and add new information to our file folders. And we can always update the information in our file folders. Sometimes a fact in a file folder might be wrong, and when we read, we can delete or change the information.

Today we are going to learn a new strategy called the Knew–New connection.

I noticed during these lessons that children frequently report loud and proud, "I knew that!" My first internal reaction was, "No you didn't. You couldn't possibly have known that!" But after some reflection, I came to the conclusion that it didn't really matter if the students were telling the truth. The purpose of the lesson is to gain awareness and understanding about background knowledge and how we build it. No matter what side of the chart the facts are recorded on, *New* or *Knew*, in the end it all becomes "Now I Know."

- Write the words on the board or have them on flash cards. Discuss the difference between the two words.
- Introduce the text you will be reading.
- Ask students to find the file on tarantulas in their brain and pull it out.
- Invite students to share the facts they already have in their file folder with a partner.
- Model what is in your file folder:

My file folder on tarantulas is not very big. I know that they are a kind of spider and they are very big and scary and poisonous, but I'm not sure if they are poisonous to humans. Maybe when I read, I'll be able to update my file. I also know that some people like them and keep them as pets.

- Explain to the students you will be reading the chapter slowly, one sentence at a time. After each sentence, you will decide if the information you just read was *New* or something that you already *Knew*.
- Read and talk through the text. Record your responses on the enlarged Knew–New Connections chart.

"Tarantulas are the largest spiders." Now I'm thinking that I knew that tarantulas were big, but I didn't know that they were the largest of all spider. So I'm going to write that fact on the *New* side.

- Continue reading, thinking aloud and recording the information on the Knew–New Connections chart.
- End the lesson:

Today, we have been learning about background knowledge and how it can help us to find new information that we can add to the file folder in our brains. Here, I have facts that I already knew about tarantulas, but here is lot of new information that I have learned from reading this book. I would like you to think for a moment—what happens to all this information now? Please turn and talk to your partner about this. I think now I can say that all this information has been added to my file folder and I can store it back inside my head. The next time I'm reading a book on tarantulas, I will be able to make more connections because my file folder is a little bigger.

The "Knew–New" Connection

Name: _____ 32.

Title: Unusual Spiders

Topic: Tarantulas

KNEW that already!	This is NEW to me!
• hairy • pets • injects venom	• largest spider • peaceful • 4 – 10 inches long (legs spread out) • female – 35 yrs male – 5 – 7 yrs • live in burrows • not poisonous to humans
↖ Now...I	KNOW! ↗

Lesson 2 (Independent Practice): My Knew–New Connections

This follow-up lesson gives students practice making the Knew–New connection on their own.

- Have each student prepare their sticky notes by labeling two with the word *KNEW* and two with the word *NEW*. These can be stuck to the surface of their desk until they are needed.
- Each student chooses a book to read.
- Have them look through their books, using the table of contents to find a section or short chapter they are interested in reading.
- Have students pair up. Each student discusses with a partner what they are reading about and what facts they already have stored inside their file folder.
- Invite the students to start reading independently and pay attention to their thinking.
- After each sentence or paragraph, the students use one of their sticky notes to label a fact as either *KNEW* or *NEW*, by writing the fact on the sticky note and flagging the place on the page.
- Once the section has been read, and all four sticky notes have been placed in the text, students go back to their partner and share their *NEW*s and *KNEW*s.
- After discussion, students peel off their sticky notes and place them on The Knew–New Connection chart. They respond to the question at the bottom of the sheet.

or

- After discussion, have students create a Now I Know sheet by drawing a picture of the subject and labeling it with facts they now know.

For this lesson you will need
- nonfiction books at or below students' reading level
Each student will need
- Knew–New Connections page (page 120)
- four sticky notes (two each of two different colors works best)

Lesson 3 (Teacher Directed/Independent Practice): Introducing Sketch Connections

For this lesson you will need
• a nonfiction book: e.g., *One Tiny Turtle* by Nicola Davies; *Our Seasons* by Grace Lin and Ranida McKneally; *The Best Book of Nighttime Animals* by Belinda Weber
• a prepared sketch of an image from the book

This simple and effective strategy, adapted from *Moving Up with Literacy Place* (2008: 68), uses sketches as the starting point for students to find connections to the information they are reading. Two different reproducibles have been provided (pages 121 and 122), and students can choose which one works best for them. Teacher modeling, as always, is the most effective way to teach the students how a strategy works.

• Begin the lesson:

We've been talking about making connections while we read and how it can help us make more sense of the information. Sometimes these connections can be to personal experiences, something that has actually happened to us before. Other times they can be background knowledge, something we already knew about the subject. Today, we're going to use sketches as a way of helping us think about our connections. I'm going to read a book called *One Tiny Turtle* by Nicola Davies. It's a book about a special kind of turtle called a Loggerhead Sea Turtle. You will see that I have already sketched one of these turtles on chart paper. As I read, I'm going to draw lines from this drawing and add my connections. I'm going to try to make sure that my connections are ones that will help me understand the information better.

• Begin to read and add connections to your sketch. Pre-reading the text before the lesson helps you to determine what connections you will share during the read-aloud.

Sketch Connections: teacher sample on *One Tiny Turtle* by Nicola Davies.

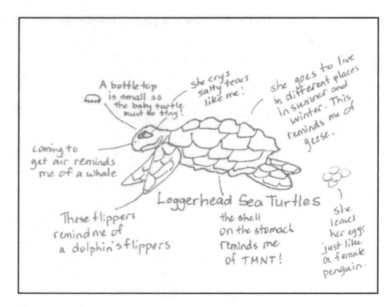

Note that five to seven connections is a good number for the read-aloud. The connection to TMNT (Teenage Mutant Ninja Turtles) is not connected to the text; I included it to model the difference between quick and deep-thinking connections.

• End the lesson:

While I was reading today, I was paying attention to the connections I was making to this book on Loggerhead Sea Turtles. I didn't know very much about these turtles before I started to read, but making connections helped me to understand the information better. But I'm wondering if all the connections I made today really helped me to understand and learn about these turtles. Can anybody see one connection that might not be really helping me with my understanding? I think you're right—thinking about Teenage Mutant Ninja Turtles does not really help to deepen my understanding of Loggerhead Sea Turtles. So I'm going to try to stay away from that kind of connection and I'd like you to try to stay away too. Remember, active readers make connections that help them understand the text better.

Lesson 4 (Independent Practice): Making Sketch Connections

For this lesson, each student will need
• a Sketch Connections 1 (page 121) or Sketch Connections 2 form (page 122)
• choice of text at or below reading level

• Have students select a book on a topic of their choice.
• Students draw or sketch a picture of the topic in the centre of the Sketch Connections 1 page. They read and add lines to their drawing, recording their connections.

or

• Students fill out the Sketch Connections 2 form, drawing and writing facts from the book and making connections.
• Students share their connections with a partner.

Lesson 5 (Teacher Modeling, Guided Practice): Expanding Connections

For this lesson you will need
• a short passage from a nonfiction book; a Big Book works well
• sticky notes
Each student will need
• a sticky note or Thinking Bubble (page 47) (optional)

Expanding connections helps readers build on their understanding of making connections. It also enables them to find sources for their connections other than personal experiences. Because nonfiction texts can often be based on content with which we have no personal experience, it is important to introduce students to different ways to make connections to information. The modeling you do gives students insight into what connecting looks and sounds like; the guided practice part of the lesson can immediately follow the modeling, or be done the next day.

• Begin the lesson:

If a student makes a connection that lacks depth, ask yourself, *Has that connection helped the student understand this text better?* If the answer is no, the student needs your support in finding a connection that is more deeply connected to the topic or context of the text.

Making connections to nonfiction texts helps readers to find meaning and make sense of what they are reading. If we can find things inside our heads that we know already, it can help us understand the topic better. Today, I'm going to read aloud a passage from this book about _____. I know a little about the subject, but not a lot. While I'm reading, I'm going to be thinking about what, in the book, reminds me of things that I have experienced or that I already know about or have seen in another book or movie. Here are some codes that I'm going to use when I'm thinking about my connections today.

(Write on chart paper or the board)

T–S	**Text-to-Self** is when I make a connection to a personal experience.
T–T	**Text-to-Text** is when I make a connection to another book, movie, or text source.
T–W	**Text-to-World** is when I make a connection to something I already know about the world from my background knowledge.

- Begin your read-aloud/think-aloud, stopping periodically when you make a connection.
- Talk through the text, using the sticky notes to record your connections and code your responses.
- If continuing the lesson the next day, remind students about the different ways we can connect to nonfiction texts: Text-to-Self, Text-to-Text, Text-to-World. Review the purpose of making connections: to help the reader better understand the text.

When Making Connections...

- Is my connection connected to the topic?
- Does my connection help me understand this information better?
- Is my connection to a personal experience, another book, or something I already knew about the world?

- Choose a nonfiction book that invites students to make many connections. Suggested topics: family, community, animals, backyard insects, weather.
- Read and share the content of one or two pages with the students. Ask them to listen to the information and find a place in the text where they made a connection.
- Reread the pages and have each student come up to place a sticky note on the page where their "thinking voice was the loudest."

or

- Ask students to turn and share their connection with a partner, telling what kind of connection they made: T–S, T–T, or T–W.
- Invite students to share their connections and record them on chart paper, including the code beside each.

Lesson 6 (Independent Practice): Expanding Connections on Your Own

For this lesson, each student will need
- choice of book, at or below reading level
- three sticky notes
- Three Kinds of Connections chart (page 123)

- Students choose their own books.
- Have students prepare their sticky notes by labeling them *T–S*, *T–T*, and *T–W*.
- Depending on grade level and length of the text, invite students to read the entire text or choose a section or chapter to read.
- While they read, students mark their connections with sticky notes.
- Students use the Three Kinds of Connections chart to record their connections.

Knew–New Connections

Name: _____ Date: _____

Title: _____ Topic:_____

I KNEW this already!	This is NEW to me!

Explain what happens to these NEW and KNEW facts now:

Sketch Connections 1

Name: _____   Date: _____

Making connections to things you already know helps you to understand information better. Sketch an image from the book. Draw lines from your sketch and add your connections.

Sketch Connections 2

Name: _____   Date: _____

Sketch and write a fact from the book.	Draw and write about your connection.
_____ _____ _____	This reminds me of _____ _____ _____
Sketch and write a fact from the book.	Draw and write about your connection.
_____ _____ _____	This reminds me of _____ _____ _____

Three Kinds of Connections

Name: _____   Date: _____

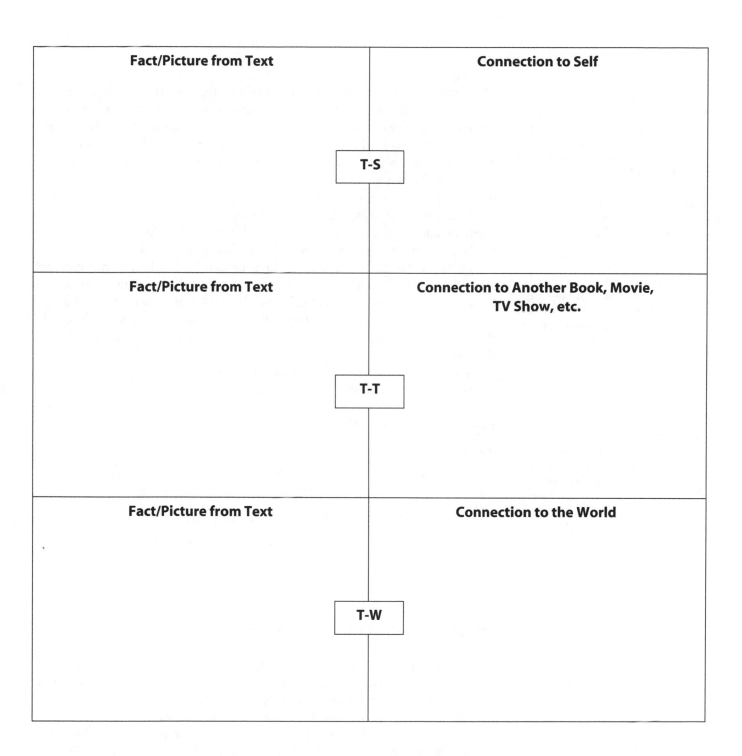

Fact/Picture from Text	Connection to Self
	T-S

Fact/Picture from Text	Connection to Another Book, Movie, TV Show, etc.
	T-T

Fact/Picture from Text	Connection to the World
	T-W

7 The Power to Transform

"In order to construct any kind of meaning in our literacy learning and our life learning, we must find ways to cull and prune the details with which we are bombarded. We must reorganize and create our own explanations for what we are learning, our own definitions of our lives at any particular juncture."— Keene & Zimmerman

The word "transforming" has its roots in the strategy of synthesizing. I changed the name of the power to Transform because I believed it to be a word more familiar to children.

"Evaluative understandings are an important branch of comprehension that often gets overlooked in nonfiction because of our focus on getting children to simply restate the facts…. In essence, they require the reader to use both literal and interpretive understandings to encourage more complex thinking."— Tony Stead (2006: 114)

The strategy of transforming comes from synthesizing. It is the last strategy I teach and one that, for me, is really a culmination of all the other strategies. Synthesizing combines awareness and understanding on all levels—it is the summary of text, combined with the readers' connections, questions, and inferences, to formulate a new perspective. While a summary is a retelling of someone else's ideas, a synthesis is a "rethinking" of your own. It is the "ah-ha" moment when something from the text and something from your thinking merge to produce an illumination or crystallization of thought. It is, in my opinion, the grand finale of understanding; a celebration of thinking. The ultimate experience in reading is when our thinking changes or is transformed in some way.

Synthesizing is challenging, and I continue to reflect and refine my approach to teaching it. I believe that, if students have learned the previous strategies and have developed an awareness of thinking along the way, moving toward insight is a natural progression (see Synthesis diagram on page 126). The key lies in defining the concept and teaching students *what* transforming is before you teach them *how* to do it.

Figuring out the difference between a summary and a synthesis was the first step in helping me understand the complexity of the strategy.

SUMMARY VS. SYNTHESIS

SUMMARY	SYNTHESIS
• "two-dimensional" reading: text + reader	• "three-dimensional" reading: text + reader's thinking = new thought
• facts from the text made smaller	• facts from the text expanded upon
• no additional input	• opinions, thoughts, ideas included
• a retelling of the text	• a rethinking of the text

Introducing the Power to Transform

I have been through many different "concept" lessons on the power to Transform. I like to use concrete examples to help the students better understand the concept. I tried using words that shared the same root, such as "synthesizer" or "synthetic fabric," then moved to examples, such as doing a jigsaw puzzle or baking, as examples of "putting together to create something new." However, something did not sit right with these examples. These examples both have an end that is known, a desired outcome. So, as much as the result is something new, there is a right or wrong way inherent in the process. The other thing that

See the list of Books for Transforming for books recommended for teacher modeling and guided practice.

wasn't sitting well with me was the word "new." I heard once that a genius, in his/her lifetime, develops an average of only 31 new thoughts. If this is the case, then it seems unrealistic to attempt to teach students that, every time they read something, they need to come up with a "new" thought or idea. This certainly doesn't happen every time I read, so how can I expect my students to? I needed to refine how I approached the concept, as I did not want to overwhelm students or present something that was not realistic in terms of their understanding or success.

My new approach when teaching the Nonfiction Reading Power to Transform is that the new thought does not need to be one that no person has ever thought before. I approach it more as a new perspective or a new way of looking at something. It may be a thought that was already in your head before you read, but now has been revisited, reevaluated, or rearranged, so that you might be looking at it from a different angle or a different perspective.

I use the example "Reduce/Reuse/Recycle," a theme of many books on the environment I use for teaching this strategy. This "message" is not something new: all children have heard this, in various ways, many times before. The process of synthesizing, or transformed thinking, is that despite the fact that that thought was already sitting in your head before you read, now the thought is permeating your thinking in a slightly different way. Now, you may actually think differently about recycling and the environment, perhaps even to the point that it may change your actions as well as your thinking.

For this lesson you will need
• the Nonfiction Reading Powers model (page 29)
• 4–6 plastic sandwich bags
• Lego™ pieces: an equal number of pieces and sizes in each bag
• a Transformer™ action figure

• Begin the lesson:

Today, we will be learning about the last Nonfiction Reading Power, or thinking power, which we call *Transforming*.

(Place Transform puzzle piece in the head of the Nonfiction Reading Powers model.)

I think of Transforming as a celebration of all the thinking that we've been learning about. It's using all your thinking together. Has anyone ever seen a Transformer™ toy before?

(Hold up action figure)

Who can tell me what it does? (changes from one thing into another). Well, it's a little like your thinking when you read. Everyone has thoughts and ideas already stored in his or her head. When you read, sometimes the ideas in the book mix with the ideas in your head, and this can sometimes change your thinking in some way.

What happens if you only move a few of the pieces of the Transformer™? (It doesn't transform completely) That's a little like your thinking too. Sometimes we learn new facts when we read, which is like moving a few pieces. But sometimes, those facts mix with our own ideas and all the pieces get moved around—and our thinking changes.

A few years ago, I read a book and it completely changed my thinking about reading. I used to think that when you read, everything you needed was in there in what you were reading, the information and answers to all the questions were right there in the book. But now I understand that the book is only half of what reading is. The other half of reading is your thinking. The book plus my thinking is what reading is.

(Draw visual on the board.)

Book   +   My thinking   = Reading

- Give a bag of Lego™ to each table group and invite students to use the pieces to construct something using all the pieces in the bag. Allow a maximum of five minutes.
- Ask the students to look around the room to see the other structures.

  What do you notice about the structures? (Every structure is different, even though everyone had the same pieces.)

- Ask the students to deconstruct, then reconstruct their pieces into a different structure.

  What do you notice? (The structures were different from the first ones, and different from each other.)

- End the lesson:

  I wanted you to use the Lego™ pieces to teach you a little bit about Transforming. Everyone had the same pieces but each group created a different structure. Then you created something new, using the same pieces. It's a little like reading and thinking. Reading can sometimes rearrange your thinking, just like you rearranged your Lego™ pieces. Sometimes, when you rearrange your thinking, you end up with a different structure to your thinking, or a different way of looking at something. Books can be that powerful—they can actually change the way you think about something. Today, everyone had the same pieces of Lego™, but you all combined the pieces differently to create different structures. It's a little like that with reading—several people could read the same piece of text, but each one could have a different transformed thought.

  Remember that not all books invite this kind of thinking. I read a lot of books and, even if I really love a book, it might not change the way I think about something. But other times, the stuff in the book and the stuff in my head come together and I think, *Whoah! I've never thought about it that way before.* What is most important is that you open yourself up to the possibilities that a book can change the way you think.

First The by Laura Vaccaro Seeger is a picture book I use during my introduction to the strategy of Transforming. The simple text and illustrations provide young readers with many examples of transformations in nature—from egg to chicken; from caterpillar to butterfly; from tadpole to frog.

Books for Transforming

Jeannie Baker, *Where the Forest Meets the Sea* (P)

Lynne Cherry, *The Great Kapok Tree* (P, I)

Nicola Davies, *Ice Bear: In the Steps of the Polar Bear* (P, I)

David Dobson, *Can We Save Them? Endangered Species of North America* (I)

Denise Fleming, *Where Once There Was A Wood* (P)

Linda Glaser, *Our Home* (P)

Steve Jenkins, *Actual Size* (P, I)

Steve Jenkins, *Almost Gone* (P, I)

Steve Jenkins, *Animals in Flight* (P, I)

Steve Jenkins, *Biggest, Fastest, Strongest* (P, I)

Steve Jenkins, *Hottest, Coldest, Highest, Deepest* (P, I)

Steve Jenkins, *I See A Kookaburra* (P, I)

Steve Jenkins, *On Top of the World* (P, I)

Steve Jenkins, *Slap, Squeak and Scatter: How Animals Communicate* (P, I)

Steve Jenkins, *What Do You Do When Someone Wants to Eat You?* (P, I)

Katharine Kenah, *The Bizarre Body* (P)

Katharine Kenah, *Space Mysteries* (P)

Katharine Kenah, *Weird and Wacky Plants* (P)

Kingfisher, *I Wonder Why There's a Hole in the Sky and Other Questions About the Environment* (P)

Kingfisher, *I Wonder Why Spiders Spin Webs – and other questions about creepy crawlies* (P)

Kingfisher, *I Wonder Why the DoDo is Dead – and other questions about animals in danger* (P)

Barbara Kerley, *A Cool Drink of Water* (P)

Barbara Kerley, *A Little Peace* (P, I)

Barbara Barbieri McGrath, *The Storm: Students of Biloxi, Mississippi Remember Hurricane Katrina* (I)

Peter Menzel, *Material World: A Global Family Portrait* (I)

Claire A. Nivola, *Planting the Trees of Kenya: The Story of Wangari Maathai* (P, I)

Fred Pearce, *Earth Then and Now: Amazing Images of Our Changing World* (I)

Stephanie St. Pierre, *What the Sea Saw* (P, I)

Shim Schimmel, *Dear Children of the Earth* (I)

Alice Schretle, *We* (I)

Laura Vaccaro Seeger, *First The* (P)

David J. Smith, *If the World Were a Village* (I) Rochelle Strauss, *One Well: The Story of Water on Earth* (I)

Rochelle Strauss, *Tree of Life: The Incredible Biodiversity of Life on Earth* (I)

Jane Breskin Zalben, *Paths to Peace: People Who Changed the World* (I)

Scaffolded Lessons for Transforming

Lesson 1 (Teacher Modeling and Guided Practice): Transforming Our Thinking

For this lesson you will need
• Transforming My Thinking (page 132) or React with Nonfiction (page 133), enlarged on a chart or overhead
• a nonfiction book; e.g., *Hottest, Coldest, Highest, Deepest*; *What Do You Do When Something Wants to Eat You?* by Steve Jenkins

Each student will need
• a Transforming My Thinking (page 132) or React with Nonfiction (page 133) sheet

Bottom line, the transforming (synthesizing) strategy is not easy to teach. It is the one strategy that many teachers initially struggle with. What determines the students' understanding of both concept and process most is the book you choose to use in modeling the strategy. I look for books that aren't dense with facts but that evoke a big reaction from the reader, a reaction that could lead to the emergence of a new perspective. Steve Jenkins is one of my favorite nonfiction authors for teaching and modeling this strategy, because he presents short simple facts, yet his books evoke big reactions from students and adults alike. He also includes some great comparisons to help children get perspective on size, speed, depth, etc.

• Begin the lesson:

Yesterday, we began to look at the Nonfiction Reading Power to Transform, the strategy that takes our thinking and kind of rearranges it—like rearranging the Lego™ pieces or the pieces on a Transformer™ toy.

Think back—when we learned about summarizing, we learned to retell the information from a text. But now, we are moving past retelling into rethinking. We are going to read and really pay attention to how our thinking changes.

Today I'm going to be reading this book that is filled with facts about the Earth. I'm going to read a page out loud. On this side of the chart, I'm going to write down the fact from the book. Then on the other side, I'm going to record my thinking. This might be a connection, a question, a visual image, or an inference.

- Read aloud one page from the book.
- Record a fact on one side of the chart, and record your reaction on the other.
- Continue same process with the next three or four pages.
- Tell the students that it's their turn. Pass out copies of Transforming My Thinking.
- Read aloud one page from the book and invite the students to record the fact and then record their thinking. Allow time for independent writing.
- Have students share their thinking with a partner.
- Read one or two more pages and have students continue to write and share.
- Continue the lesson:

Now that we've finished reading and summarizing the facts about the Earth and adding our thoughts, I want to think about how reading this book may have changed our thinking in some way. Remember, I don't want to just write down a new fact that I've learned here. That would be like I just moved around a few pieces of my Transformer™ toy. I want to write down a bigger idea. I want to move all the pieces so that I have a completely new perspective about the Earth.

I sometimes like to think about the person who wrote the book and ask myself, *Why did this author want me to read this book?* This book had a lot of facts about the Earth. We could read this book and then I could test you on all the facts, numbers, and names from the book. But I don't think Steve Jenkins wrote this book because he wanted us to memorize facts. I think he wrote this book because he wanted each one of us to rethink some ideas about the Earth. How has my thinking about the earth changed?

- Invite the students to write their new thinking on the bottom of their page.
- Fill in the *My Transformed Thought* on the modeling chart, but don't show the students until they have had time to write their own.
- Invite students to share with a partner, then share out.
- Reveal your own Transformed Thought.
- End the lesson:

The Nonfiction Reading Power to Transform is thinking about something that we read in a new way. It's taking ideas from the book and ideas from our heads and really trying to figure out how putting those ideas together can change the way we view something.

Adapting the lesson for primary students is a way of scaffolding the process for them. I like to begin with a simplified approach at first, focusing on the difference between the "fact from the book" and the "idea in my head." Reading aloud simple nonfiction books that are filled with interesting facts work well for this lesson, and often produce a collective "Wow!"

Transforming My Thinking samples: Grade 4 on *What Do You Do When Something Wants to Eat You?* by Steve Jenkins; Grade 6 on *Hottest, Coldest, Highest, Deepest* by Steve Jenkins.

Sample 1 (Grade 4)

Title: What Do You Do When Something Eats You? — Topic: Cameron — 41.

Facts: What I know so far.... (V.I.P.'s only)	My Thinking Voice: My reaction/response: (What I'm thinking, wondering, feeling...)
Octopus shoot ink	I knew that! (I'm smart!) Is it washable or permanint. Can you write with it? Does it smell? Does it hurt?
Clown fish hide in poisun plants.	Hey! That's NEMO! (Nemo) That's pretty sneaky. Maybe I will hide in poisun eye-ve Why doesn't Nemo get poisund?
glass snake is a lizard. Tail brakes and wiggles away	Cool! That's gross! Why is it called a snake? How long do they wiggle?

Synthesis:
My new thoughts: What is not written in the text, but now I'm thinking about (The part that "sticks")

I didn't know how smart animals are but believ me their smart! I wonder how they know what to do? Good Job or else they'd all get eaten.

agear 2005

Sample 2 (Grade 6)

Title: Hottest, Coldest, Highest, Deepest — Topic: Earth Facts

Facts: What I know so far...	My Thinking Voice: My reaction/response: (What I'm thinking, wondering, feeling...)
• Atacama Dessert - driest place on earth Child	• That is amazing! I wonder if anyone survived in the desert? I can't believe it didn't rain for 400 years!
• Marianas Trench-deepest part of the ocean ↓ Philippines	• That is deep, how do they know how deep it is? When I swam at the Philippnes, I never knew I was swimming near the deepest ocean trench!

My transformed thought:
My "after reading thought" – what the author did not actually write but now I'm thinking. (The part that matters most to me; the part that "sticks")

First, I was thinking this is just one of those normal books about facts, but now after, when I finish it is getting me to think about things in life that is extraordinary in the world.

React with Nonfiction: Grade 1 sample on *I Wonder Why Spiders Spin Webs* (Kingfisher)

Synthesizing Non Fiction

Fact	Reaction
• wasps chew their food	• I didn't know that wasps could chew-like us
2 • Honeybees wings beat 200 times per second	• I can't see that in my mind.
3 • a insect has a skeleton out side there body	• I think I'd rather have bones.
4 • there are 900,000 kinds of insects!	• I wonder how many kinds of snakes there are?
Name	Great thinking ★

Lesson 2 (Guided and Independent Practice): How My Thinking Changes

It takes a lot of practice to be aware of new thinking. Students will need many opportunities to synthesize and transform. One of the simplest ways we can teach students to transform is by allowing them to notice their thinking before and after reading. Moving to books that evoke issues such as animal extinction, global warming, water conservation, etc. (see Books for Transforming list on page 127) allows readers to learn new information about the world—information that may, in turn, change the way they think or act.

• Begin the lesson:

When you read, ideas from the book and ideas from your head merge together. When you read nonfiction, you learn new facts and information. Sometimes this new information helps you to understand a little better something you already

For this lesson you will need
• a nonfiction book on an issue: *A Cool Drink of Water* by Barbara Kerley for Primary; *One Well: The Story of Water* on Earth by Rochelle Strauss for Intermediate (Intermediate teachers may choose to share both books with the class and discuss similarities and differences in the messages.)
Each student will need
• How My Thinking Changes (Primary) sheet (page 134) or How My Thinking Changes (Intermediate) sheet (page 135)

knew. Other times, the new information changes you in some way, makes you think about something in a new way, or gives you a new perspective. To me, the most powerful part about reading information is not just learning a bunch of new facts; it is when my thinking changes because of what I read.

Today we're going to read a book about water. I'd like you to all think about the topic. Find your file folder of facts and your chapters of experience and see what's already in your head. What do you know about water? I'm looking for more than just "It's wet," and "You can drink it." Please think about water on the earth, water supply, and how water affects life on earth.

A recommended pair of books for this lesson that focus on the environmental impact of housing development and clear-cutting: *Where Once There Was a Wood* by Denise Fleming (Primary); *The Great Kapok Tree* by Lynne Cherry (Intermediate).

- Invite students to find a partner and share their thoughts about water.
- Pass out How My Thinking Changes sheets and ask students to jot down some thoughts about water on the top section of the page.
- Now ask them to think about what questions they have about water, and invite them to record their questions on the second section. Have them share questions with a partner
- Continue the lesson:

Now I'm going to read this book to you. I'd like you to listen to the words and notice how the ideas from the book and ideas you already have fit together. Notice if any of your ideas about water on the earth change as I'm reading.

- Read the book aloud.

Now that the book is finished, I'd like you to ask yourself, "How has my thinking changed?" You may have learned some interesting new facts about water, but more than that, how has this book changed your understanding? Has this book made you think about water in a different way? Why do you think the author wrote this book?

"Turn and talk" provides an opportunity for students to practice their thinking out loud before they begin to write, as well as a chance to hear the ideas of others.

- Have students turn and share their ideas with a partner.
- Then have them write their ideas on the last section of the sheet.
- End the lesson:

Sometimes noticing our thinking is important when we read, because it means that we are not just reading the words that someone else wrote, but we are also adding our own ideas and thoughts into the book. Not all books are going to change the way you think about something. In fact, often I read a book for pleasure and just enjoy the words. But sometimes I might read a book like the one we read today and, after I put the book away, it stays with me. I might think about this book the next time I turn on my tap and let the water run while I brush my teeth… because now I realize that there is not an endless supply of water on earth. I might feel more appreciative of where I live, knowing that in some places people have to walk a long distance every day just to get water.

What's important to remember is that reading and thinking go together, and sometimes reading can even change your thinking.

How My Thinking Changes: Primary sample on *A Cool Drink of Water* by Barbara Kerley; Intermediate sample on *One Well* by Rochelle Strauss.

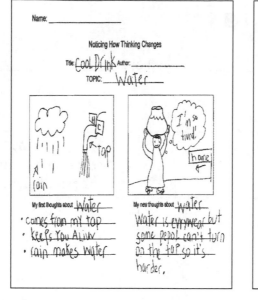

Name: _____

Noticing How Thinking Changes

Title: Cool Drink   Author: _____

TOPIC: Water

My first thoughts about Water
- comes from my top
- keeps you Aliuv
- rain makes water

My new thoughts about water
Water is everywear but some pepol can't turn on the top so it's harder.

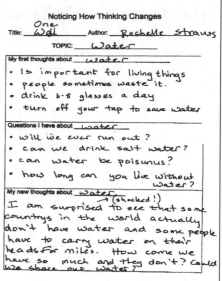

Noticing How Thinking Changes

Title: One Well   Author: Rochelle Strauss

TOPIC: Water

My first thoughts about water
- Is important for living things
- people sometimes waste it.
- drink 6-8 glasses a day
- turn off your tap to save water

Questions I have about water
- will we ever run out?
- can we drink salt water?
- can water be poisunus?
- how long can you live without water?

My new thoughts about water → (shocked!)
I am surprised to see that some countrys in the world actually don't have water and some people have to carry water on their heads for miles. How come we have so much and they don't? Could we share our water?

Transforming My Thinking

Title: _____   Author : _____

Summary Facts from the text.	My Thinking Voice My connections, questions, inferences, visual images, thoughts, reactions, feelings, etc.

My Transformed Thought
What is my new thinking?
Facts from the book + My thinking = Something that I may not have ever thought about before, but now I am thinking about.

React with Nonfiction

Name: _____   Date: _____

Title: _____   Author: _____

Fact (What's in the book)	React (What's in my head)

How My Thinking Changes (Primary)

Name: _____

Title: _____

Topic: _____

Date: _____

Author: _____

My first thoughts about _____

My new thoughts about _____

How My Thinking Changes (Intermediate)

Name: _____ Date: _____

Title: _____ Author: _____

Topic: _____

My first thoughts about _____

Questions I have about _____

My new thoughts about _____

8 Application and Assessment

The best thing about teaching is that it ends. Every June we say goodbye to our students and our colleagues, and we close up shop for a while. While everything is still fresh in your mind, June is a good time for reflecting on what worked, what didn't work, and what things you want to change or add for the next school year, as the hectic pace of the first weeks of September don't lend themselves well for reflection or planning.

Fitting It All In

Give yourself permission to slow down and not rush through everything you want to cover in a year.

I am often asked by teachers "How do you fit it all in? How do you teach all the Reading Powers and cover all your content areas? Do you focus on fiction and nonfiction at the same time?" I have come to believe that it is better to cover fewer things well in a year than cover many things poorly.

When planning my year, I like to divide our ten teaching months into five two-month chunks. This way, I can choose a content focus for each chunk, making the school year plan more manageable. This might mean, for example, that staffs work together for a two-month period on the scope and sequence for teaching the Nonfiction Reading Power strategies and the Nonfiction writing forms. Planning in chunks is a way for me to think about linking literacy to content areas, and covering them at the same time during the year. I like to begin the year, for example, with the Connect power, as it helps me get to know my students and builds a sense of community. This links with teaching personal narrative in writing, where students are writing their chapter, prompted by the Connect books. It also works well to link this to a social studies unit on the community.

Taking time to create a year plan (see page 139) helps me keep my lessons in check and nudges me to wrap things up when it's time to move on.

Reflecting and Planning

Planning and brainstorming a year plan can be done individually or with a colleague who teaches the same grade.

1. Reflect on your current practice. What's working? What things would you like to change? Add? (See Reflections and Plans, page 137, for an organizer you might find useful.)

2. Brainstorm specific literacy areas you want to focus on in Reading and Writing. Remember to be realistic—you can't teach everything! Use Planning My Year (page 138) to organize your thoughts.

3. Divide your year into five two-month chunks (see Year Plan form on page 139). Each chunk will have a literacy focus, a content area focus, and a math focus.

Reflections and Plans

Name: _____   Date: _____

This/last year, I took some risks and made positive changes to my literacy practice by implementing (e.g., new assessment tools; comprehension instruction; modeling think-alouds; the use of assessment to guide my teaching; nonfiction writing; guided reading; etc.)

-
-
-

In reflecting upon my year, I am most proud of

-
-
- \

I feel I still need to work on

-
-
-

Looking ahead to next year, I would like to continue on my path of best literacy practice by attempting to integrate this/these into my literacy program:

-
-
-

The most recent professional book I read that affected my teaching:

-

Next on my "must read" list of professional resources:

-

-

Planning My Year

Name: _____   Date: _____

What do I want to cover? (Brainstorm)

Writing

✓

✓

✓

Reading

✓

✓

✓

Fiction Strategies	Nonfiction Strategies

Social Studies

✓

✓

✓

Science

✓

✓

✓

Math

✓

✓

✓

Year Plan

Name: _____

Date: _____

Month	Reading	Writing	Social Studies	Science	Math
Sept.–Oct.	Focus: _____	Focus: _____	Focus: _____	Focus: _____	Focus: _____
Nov.–Dec.	Focus: _____	Focus: _____	Focus: _____	Focus: _____	Focus: _____
Jan.–Feb.	Focus: _____	Focus: _____	Focus: _____	Focus: _____	Focus: _____
March–April	Focus _____	Focus: _____	Focus: _____	Focus: _____	Focus: _____
May–June	Focus: _____	Focus: _____	Focus: _____	Focus: _____	Focus: _____

4. Consider how your week is structured and block off at least two periods a week for specific comprehension instruction or Reading Power time.

5. Consider the social studies and science topics that you will be covering within the year. Use the chart below to link up each Nonfiction Reading Power with a possible content area. While our goal is that students be able to use any of the Reading Powers with any subject area, some content topics lend themselves more readily to certain strategies.

Nonfiction Reading Power	Suggested Content Area Links
Zoom-In	Life Cycles, Weather, Plants, Animals, Mapping
Question/Infer	Animals, Space, Weather, Extreme Environments, Force and Motion, Electricity
Determine Importance	History, Biography, Human Body, Global Warming, Weather, Space
Connect	All About Me, Family and Community, Weather, Seasons, People Around the World, Cultural Diversity, Biography
Transform	Environment, Global Warming, Endangered Animals, Recycling, Global Citizenship, Biography, History

Assessment

"The only way we can confidently assess our students' comprehension is when they share their thinking with us. Readers reveal their comprehension by responding to text, not by answering a litany of literal questions at the end of the chapter on rocks and minerals."—Harvey & Goudvis (2000: 189)

"Effective assessment provides you and your students with information to improve reading comprehension…. As well, useful assessment presents you with detailed and dependable information to guide instruction and learning in the classroom."—Faye Brownlie and Sharon Jeroski (2006: 7)

Reading instruction has changed considerably since I was in school. The goal of reading is no longer "saying the words right" and "getting the answer right." We are now working toward the goals of students enhancing understanding, acquiring knowledge, and constructing meaning. Granted, assessment of the outdated goals proved to be much more cut and dried and, to some degree, easier to determine: you either said the word correctly or you didn't; you either got the answer right or you didn't. Assessing students' comprehension now requires a great deal more objectivity, metacognitive understanding, and time.

If our goal is for our students to become "thinkers" of text, then the only way we can confidently assess our students' comprehension is when they share their thinking with us. Assessing our students' thinking happens over time, not in a single sitting twice a year. Baseline information collected at the beginning of the year is imperative for guiding instruction, but regular informal assessments throughout the year are often the most effective way of gathering evidence of your students' "thinking journey." By listening to your students, asking them questions, and watching them closely as they interact with text, you are able to notice which comprehension strategies they activate to make meaning and which ones they lack. We need to witness how our students keep track of their thinking and how they are able to demonstrate understanding with specific evidence. This evidence comes in a variety of forms—oral and written, formal and informal. We can find out if readers are using comprehension strategies by using the following forms of assessment.

LISTENING FOR EVIDENCE OF APPLICATION

Students may begin to use the "language of thinking" without prompts, in many different areas of thinking and learning. Keep in mind, however, that using the language isn't enough, evidence of substance is essential.

LISTENING TO "PARTNER TALK"

Many of the lessons in this book include partner sharing. Students may engage in quick or deep-thinking responses. Circulating the room and listening in during this sharing time is valuable in determining those who may need more support in going deeper with their thinking.

CONFERRING WITH STUDENTS

A written response is rarely an accurate reflection of a student's ability to think. Individual reading conferences still rank as the most valuable venue for determining your students' understanding. The personal responses given during these one-on-one conversations are the clearest windows into your students' thinking. You may be surprised at how even your most reluctant student can open up, if they are asked the right question in the right setting.

INDEPENDENT WRITTEN ASSESSMENT

While I value informal conversations and observations, there is still a need for some kind of written response and baseline collection. These written assessments, however, should be open-ended and provide opportunities for students to demonstrate both their understanding of strategic reading and their use of specific strategies. For those students who are not able to demonstrate thinking with written output, it is only fair that they be given these assessments orally and responses be scribed. Remember, we are assessing thinking and understanding, not writing.

Ongoing assessment is important, so I encourage you to vary both the format and delivery of the assessment so that those students who might have difficulty expressing their thoughts in writing have an opportunity to share their thinking orally, and vice versa.

Three assessment forms have been provided: Sharing Your Thinking 1, 2, and 3 (pages 143–149). They provide students with an opportunity to share their understanding of the Nonfiction Reading Power strategies as well as to demonstrate the application of the strategy while reading a short piece of text. The multi-purpose design allows you to use them either during an individual conference with a student, where student responses can be scribed by the teacher directly onto the sheet, or for an independent written response. Sharing Your Thinking 1 and 2 can be completed in a single session. Sharing Your Thinking 3 can be given as a complete assessment, or can be broken down and given after each strategy has been taught. Evidence from all types of assessment—observation, oral, and written—can be gathered and used to assess where your students are and to help guide your instruction. (See Assessment Rubric for Nonfiction Reading Power on pages 150–151.)

Other Resources for Comprehension Assessment

Comprehension Toolkit: Language and Lessons for Active Literacy, Stephanie Harvey and Anne Goudvis (Heinemann): Teachers guide, reproducible short nonfiction text passages, lessons, BLMs; Primary and Intermediate toolkit available.

Reading and Responding: Evaluation Resources for Your Classroom, by Sharon Jeroski, Faye Brownlie & Linda Kaser (Nelson): Individual softcover binders for individual grades; Includes lessons, reproducible texts and assessment rubrics.

Whole Class Reading Assessment, by Jennifer Gardner & Cathie Peters (SD #73 Kamloops): Fall and spring assessments for Grades 4–7; Includes short reproducible passages, response grids, and assessment rubrics.

Sharing Your Thinking 1

Name: _____   Date: _____

Title: _____   Author: _____

Zoom In	**Main Idea**
Create a text feature to show something you learned from this text.	What is the main idea of this piece? Write some key words and use the words to write a summary.
Connect	**Question/Infer**
What connections can you make from this article? Sketch something from the article and label it with some of your connections.	What are you wondering about the article? Write your questions and then answer them from information in the text or make an inference. Questions: Inference:

Transform
How has your thinking changed? What new thoughts do you have now?

Sharing Your Thinking 2

Name: _____   Date: _____

Before you read, look carefully at the nonfiction features (headings, captions, graphs, photos, etc.). These features can tell you a lot about what the text is about.

Before you read
Predictions: What you think this article might be about?

Questions: What are you wondering about this article?

While you read
Connections: What do you already know about this topic? Write any background knowledge you might have.

Connections: What personal connections can you make to this article? Does it remind you of anything you have experienced?

Questions: What are you wondering while you read?

Inferring: Add your thinking while you read. Write a statement beginning with "Maybe…" or "I think…"

After reading
Main Idea: What is the main idea of this article? Write a summary and draw a quick sketch that might help you remember what is important.

Transform: What ideas or thoughts do you have now, that you didn't have before you read this? Why do you think the author wanted you to read this?

Sharing Your Thinking 3

Name: _____   Date: _____

Zoom-In

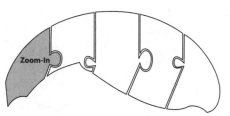

Can you name some text features that you might find in a nonfiction book?	List of text features:
Why are text features used in nonfiction books?	Explain the purpose of text features:
Look at these text features. Explain what they mean. (Give two or three examples of text features studied.)	Explain:
Read the paragraph. Create/draw a text feature to represent the information. Supply a short piece of informational text.	Text feature:

Sharing Your Thinking 3, continued

Name: _____   Date: _____

Question/Infer

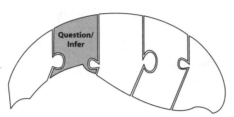

What is the title of this article?	Title:
Turn the title into a question.	Question from title:
What questions do you have before you start to read?	Questions before:
What are you wondering about while you read?	Questions during:
What information is not included but you are thinking about? Make a "Maybe…" or "I think…" statement about something that is not included in the article but that now you are thinking about.	Inferences:

Sharing Your Thinking 3, continued

Name: _____   Date: _____

Determine Importance

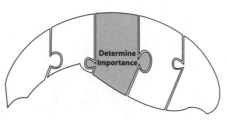

Why do readers need to be able to determine what is important in nonfiction texts?	Explain:
What is text structure? Can you name some different text structures?	Explain:
What is the text structure of this article? (Give a short nonfiction article.)	Text Structure:
Read this passage. Choose 6–8 key words that you feel are most important.	Key Words:
Use the key words to write a summary of the article.	Summary:
Draw a quick sketch of something important from the article and label it.	Sketch
How does sketching help you remember what is important?	Explain:

Sharing Your Thinking 3, continued

Name: _____   Date: _____

Connect

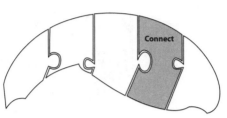

Active readers make connections when they read. What is connecting?	Explain Connecting:
Is there a place in the article where you find yourself making a personal connection? (Give short nonfiction article.)	Connection to personal experience:
Is there a place in the article where you read something that you already knew?	Connection to background knowledge:
How did making connections help you to understand this information better?	Explain:

Sharing Your Thinking 3, continued

Name: _____   Date: _____

Transform

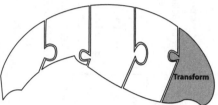

Sometimes readers' thinking can be transformed by what they read. What does this mean?	Explain Transforming:
Can you find a part in this article where your thinking changed? How did your thinking change? (Give short nonfiction article.)	Explain the change in your thinking: At first I thought… But now I'm thinking…
What idea from this article will stick with you?	Main idea:
Why do you think the author wanted you to read this article?	Reason:

Assessment Rubric for Nonfiction Reading Power

	Emergent Not Meeting	Beginning Approaching	Developing Meeting	Well Developed Fully Meeting	Fully Developed Exceeding
Zoom-In (Text Features)	Can point out some text features on a page.	Can identify some text features by name and can locate some features in the book.	Can identify and locate several text features and is able to gain some information from them. Understands the purpose of text features.	Can identify and locate several text features and is able to gain some information from them. Understands the purpose of text features. Is able to represent information using simple features.	Can identify and locate several text features and is able to gain information from them. Understands the purpose of text features. Is able to represent information using simple text features. Is able to read and represent the information using a variety of text features.
Question/Infer	Is not able to form a question about the text.	Has difficulty asking questions about the text and is able to answer questions with only one- or two-word answers.	Is able to ask simple questions from the text and is able to answer literal questions accurately. Can make some simple inferences.	Can ask questions that go beyond a literal interpretation, that reflect and invite inferences and deepen understanding. Understands that inferences are the "maybes" readers add to text when information might be missing. Questions and inferences are relevant to topic.	Can ask questions that go beyond a literal interpretation, that reflect and invite inferences and deepen understanding. Questions are exceptionally thoughtful and demonstrate a deep understanding of text. Understands that inferences are the "maybes" readers add to text when information might be missing. Can clearly explain what an inference is. Inferences are thoughtful and evidence that text, knowledge, and experiences are supporting the inference. Questions and inferences are relevant to topic.

	Emergent Not Meeting	Beginning Approaching	Developing Meeting	Well Developed Fully Meeting	Fully Developed Exceeding
Determining Importance	May be able to identify the topic.	Can identify the topic and retell some accurate facts.	Can identify topic and retell important ideas and some details. Can identify some key words.	Identifies main ideas and key words. Is able to summarize in own words. Locates specific relevant details. Is developing an awareness of text structure.	Identifies main ideas and key words. Is able to summarize in own words. Locates specific relevant details. Is developing an awareness of text structure. Understands text structure and is able to identify different text structures.
Connecting	Is unable to make connections to the text.	Claims to be making a connection, but the connections are often not related to the meaning or topic.	Can make both personal connections and connections to background knowledge when reading nonfiction. Connections are relevant to content.	Is able to make T–S, T–T, T–W connections. Can articulate how the connections have helped deepen understanding. (BIBB)	Is able to make T–S, T–T, T–W connections. Can articulate how the connections have helped enhance understanding. Demonstrates a strong understanding of connecting to text and is able to bring those connections back to the text to deepen understanding.
Transforming	Is not able to identify new thinking. May be able to retell but not rethink the text.	Is able to recognize the difference between "in the book" and "in my head" thinking. Can retell a fact and react to it.	Understands that readers sometimes develop new thoughts from reading. Is able to apply some of the reading powers to nonfiction text. New thinking might be shown only with new facts.	Can apply reading powers independently. Understands that transforming is a new way of thinking about something. Shows evidence of some retelling and rethinking when reading. Is able to articulate simple ways of rethinking the text.	Can apply reading powers independently. Understands that Transform is a new way of thinking about something. Shows evidence of some retelling and rethinking when reading. Is able to find simple ways of rethinking the text. Is able to distinguish between the text and thinking. Uses experiences and text to identify a new perspective or thought that enhances meaning and deepens understanding.

Final Thoughts

"Smart is not something you are—it's something you get. And you get smart by reading, writing, talking, listening, and investigating: by THINKING!"—Stephanie Harvey (International Reading Association Conference, Atlanta 2008)

Teaching students how to become independent strategic readers and thinkers is our destination. Reading and making sense of information books has been the vessel upon which we have been sailing. The journey we embark upon with our students proves challenging at times, other times rewarding, but ultimately as important as our arrival. Once docked, we help our students off our ship and our journey together ends. We can only hope that they leave us with all that is necessary to successfully read and think into the world.

By reading, reflecting, sharing, and learning new ways to support your students' comprehension, you are making the effort to ensure your ship is steady; that you have a dependable crew accompanying you; that you've researched well the maps, the tides, and the weather; and that you know what direction you are headed. It has been a privilege to have been able to share a small part of that journey with you.

Acknowledgments

Once again, this book could not have been written without the support and guidance of an enormous number of people. I would like to acknowledge, with deep gratitude, the many teachers, literacy support teachers, district consultants, teacher librarians, administrators, and district superintendents throughout the province of British Columbia who have supported Reading Power. Had it not been for the continued efforts of these educators towards effective comprehension instruction in classrooms and schools, and a dedication to best literacy practice, Reading Power would not exist.

First, in my own district of Vancouver, BC, I would like to thank the amazing literacy team with whom I have worked for the past three years: Meredyth Kezar, Barb McBride, Jodi Carson, Carol O'Malley, Krista Forbes, Kimberly Matterson, Liisa House, Heidi Clark, Janis Myers, Fabienne Goulet, Dianna Mezzarrobba, Carla Freisen, Marzena Michalowska, Shelagh Maguire, Dale Severyn, and Moira Ekdaul. Special thank you to the amazing Pat Dymond for her masterful skills in organizing, typing, and formatting many of my original BLMs. I respect and admire your passion for literacy and learning, and have learned so much from each of you.

Throughout the Vancouver school district, my thanks go out to the many teachers who have worked tirelessly to make literacy learning more meaningful for their students; to the teacher-librarians who have supported their efforts through purchasing and organizing recommended books, and who share in the pursuit of best literacy practice; and to the administrators who support literacy throughout their schools. While it is not possible to name them all, I would like to acknowledge a few individuals who have been instrumental in planting the Reading Power seeds in their classrooms, libraries, and schools: Donna

Boardman (Mackenzie); Jodi Carson, Joan Jung, Pat Munton (Carleton); Jo-anne Dale (Maple Grove); Carrie Gelson and Janice Parry (Seymour); Pam Broman, Suzanne Morgan, Surinder Deo (Techumsea); Joanna Wood and John Dryer (Southlands); Krista Forbes and Laura Carle (Laurier Annex); Brenda Boylan and Debbie Sunnus (Roberts Annex); Kathryn Buchan (Douglas); Nickey Mey (Champlain Heights); Bernice Jay and Mary-Anne Yu (Osler); Ian Judson (McKecknie); Judy Reitenbach, Lorraine Bayne, Donna Deltorre, Andre Lechner, Chris Hoffman (Selkirk); Georgina Arntzen, Bill Hood, Diana Wort (McQuinna); Jackie Hall, Jeanette Mumford, Mary Cottrell (Sexsmith); Jim Harcott (Kitchener); Wendy Cameron and Denise Johnson (Wolfe); Connie Robson and Erin Gibbs (Brock); Birgid Lehmann (Nightingale); Kathy Pickford (University Hill); Denise North (Killarney); Jan Miko (Beaconsfield); Bill Barrie, Delma Campbell, Besty Surchin (Norquay); Miranda Winn (Nelson); Yvette Cassidy (Van Horne); Susan Wagner and Joylene Minato (Cunningham), Sue Stevenson (Mt. Pleasant).

Of the many benefits to presenting workshops across the province of British Columbia, it is the relationships I have formed with teachers, consultants, administrators, and directors of instruction who share the same passion for literacy and learning that makes it particularly fulfilling. Many of these people have been instrumental in bringing Reading Power into their schools and districts. While unable to mention them all, I would like to acknowledge the support of Judy Dunn (Kamloops); Katherine Eades (Terrace); Kristi Clifton and Anne Dobson (Prince Rupert); Alison Sidow (Gold Trail); Caroline Catalano and Norma Heart (Trail); Judy Scott and Heather Rose (Penticton); Brenda Bell (Kelowna); Kathie Peters, Jennifer Gardner, Deanna Michaud, Linda Henney (Vernon); Lori Robinson (Merritt); Sandra Huggett (Prince George); Michelle Miller-Gauthier (Vanderhoof); Bev Young (Bulkley Valley); Michelle Lesage (Cranbrook); Rob Carmichael, Edward "Woody" Bradford, Donna Wright, Corinna Campbell, Sheilagh Burns, Kim Kass, Dave Gottschalk, Luigi DeMarzo, Bob Voth (Abbotsford); Judy Matthot, Angela Meredith, Kelly Chow, Sheilagh Pace (Burnaby); Susan MacDonald, Cheryl Edge-Partington, Nancy Gordon, Grace Sproul (Delta); Mary Philpot (Mission); Wendy Woodhurst (Salmon Arm); Bev Craig (Sunshine Coast); Allan Douglas (Comox); Barbara Illerbrun (Powell River); Kathy Moslin (Grand Forks); Laura Grills, Suki Lalli, Glen Hilder, Shelagh Lim, Heather Briske, Jackie Howard, Shelley Boone, Dave Price, Laureen Boulet (Surrey); Julie Robins, Sandra-Lynn Shortall, Marlene Mitchell (West Vancouver); Nancy Carl, Kyme Wylie, Gloria Gustavson (Coquitlam); Cheryl Burian, Janice Novakowski, Carol Saundry, Carole Wilson, Gina Rae, Jean Adshead, Sara Loat, Leslie Sobotin, Nicole Kusch, Jane MacMillan, Ted Lim, Dianne Tijmann, Gillian Partridge (Richmond); Cindy Gordon, Freda Morgan, Bonnie Stacy (Victoria); Diane Hart and Sharon Broatch (Whistler); Lori Harris and Mandy Richmond (Collingwood Jr. School); Stephanie Yorath, Susan Van Blarcom, Stella Araujo (Croften House); Lisa Chang (St. John's School); Tracy MacLeod and Ciara Corcoran (West Point Grey Academy); Kristi Crowe, Wendy West (Nelson).

Having teachers use some of my ideas as springboards for their own lessons is inspiring. A huge thank-you to the many teachers who have contributed lessons, BLMs, book titles, assessment ideas: Janice Novakowski, Krista Forbes, Heather Rose, Gillian Partridge, Jodi Carson, Carol O'Malley, Jan Wells, Janine Reid, Brenda Boylan, David Goulet, Heather Briske, Shelagh Lim, Cheryl Burian, and

Laurie Desautles. A special thank-you to Janice Novakowski for her vision, innovation, and leadership of the Richmond Primary Teachers' Study Group: Gillian Partridge, Sarah Loat, Lisa Schwartz, and Michelle Hikida, among others. Their interest and exploration of these thinking strategies into all areas of learning has been inspirational. Janice's work has inspired and influenced me enormously and I am grateful for her advice and assistance, in particular her contributions to book lists, lessons, and assessment, and her expertise in math and science. A special thank you to Heather Rose, Literacy Helping Teacher in Penticton, for her dedication to supporting teachers and students, for sharing her amazing lessons with me, and for helping me through several bouts of writer's block. Finally, I am extremely grateful to my "book list consultants"—Krista Forbes, Janice Novakowski, and Cheryl Burian—who, through many conversations, phone calls, and e-mails, helped me to organize the book lists into a useful framework.

This past year, I had the privilege of working closely with a group of teacher leaders from Gold Trail school district as they went deeper with Reading Power and became literacy coaches in their schools. These teachers reflected, questioned, took risks, developed, and shared amazing lessons with their colleagues and each other. Thank you for inviting me to be part of your learning journey: Patrice Barth, Max Beckett, Teresa Downs, Amber Horne, Leanne Lane, Jo Medley, Colleen Minnabarriet, Aislinn Mulholland, Ken Oakes, Pam Ratch, Deb Ralston, and Susan Schalles.

I would like to acknowledge, with thanks, the students around the province who have generously welcomed me into their classrooms and allowed me to share my lessons and ideas about thinking and reading. They have responded with incredible insight and enthusiasm, confirming my belief that children are far more capable than are sometimes given credit and have taught me more about reading and thinking than I could ever teach them.

I would like to recognize with gratitude and appreciation the staff at Vancouver Kidsbooks, in particular Phyllis Simon, whom I adore. They continue to provide teachers, libraries, and schools with the highest quality of children's literature and professional resources, and have been instrumental in supplying recommended Reading Power books to far corners of the province. I would also like to acknowledge with appreciation the staff of United Library Services in Burnaby, particularly Elizabeth Graves, Gloria Wong, and Nadia Fortuna. They have worked tirelessly, supporting and promoting Reading Power and supplying teachers with the recommendations from my various book lists. I feel like a kid in a candy shop whenever I visit their warehouse, but am always treated like a queen.

To my book club friends—Cheryl, Laura, Anna, Heather, Bonnie, Stella, Laura, Krista, Maria, Jarma, and Melanie—who patiently listen while I "share my thinking" about the books we read: I am blessed to have a time and a place each month that brings together great friends and great books, and am grateful for the fact that we've been together six years and have yet to make a diorama.

A very special thank you to Judy Wilbert for spreading the Reading Power word throughout her district in Wichita, Kansas, and for being the "happy ending" to my rather sad first book signing at the IRA conference in Atlanta.

To Mary Macchiusi, publisher at Pembroke, and a true friend: thank you for believing in me once again, for cheering me on to the finish line and supporting me through hills, valleys, and book signings! To Kat, my amazing editor: thank you, once again, for taking my wordy manuscript and organizing and refining it with such clarity.

Special thanks to my dearest friend, Cheryl Burian, my Atlanta sidekick, my fashion consultant, and the person with whom I am able to share all the chapters of my life, from profound sorrow to the deepest of belly laughs—I am blessed to have you as my friend.

Love and thanks to my family, in particular my mum Sheila Gear, who has shown me that, regardless of how many "chapters" fade, the ones that remain steadfast and clear are those embedded in love. Thank you to my two sisters, Janet and Alison, who were the dearest chapters of my childhood and remain an integral part of my life story. Finally, I am forever grateful to my late father, William Irvine Gear. Among the many gifts he left me, none have had more impact on my life's journey than his dedication to teaching and learning, and his passion for literature, language, poetry, and words.

And finally, my deepest love and gratitude to the "men" in my life: my husband, Richard Gatzke, who continues to support me in all aspects of my life, patiently tolerates my "busy brain" and has willingly and unselfishly allowed me to pursue this journey; and my precious boys, Spencer and Oliver—thank you for adding the richest and most meaningful chapters to my story. Seeing your sweet faces each day is all I will ever need.

Resources

Children's Book References

Banyai, Istvan (1998) *Zoom* (Puffin)

— (1998) *ReZoom* (Puffin)

Bingham, Caroline (2003) *Whales and Dolphins.*(DK Publishing)

Carle, Eric (1988)*The Very Busy Spider* (Puffin)

Cherry, Lynne (2000)*The Great Kapok Tree: A Tale of the Amazon Forest* (Voyager Books)

Clibbon, Meg & Lucy (2002) *Imagine You're a Pirate* (Annick Press)

— (2003) *Imagine You're a Wizard* (Annick Press)

— (2003) *Imagine You're a Mermaid* (Annick Press)

Davies, Nicola (2008) *One Tiny Turtle* (Candlewick Press)

de Paola, Tomie (2000)*Nana Upstairs, Nana Downstairs* (Putnam Juvenile)

Fanelli, Sarah (1995) *My Map Book* (Harper-Collins)

Fleming, Denise (2000) *Where Once There Was a Wood* (Henry Holt)

Henson, Ned (2000) *Unusual Spiders*, in the Take Two series (WrightGroup/McGraw-Hill)

Hoban, Tana (2003) *I Wonder* (Harcourt)

Hodge, Deborah (2004)*Ants* (Kids Can Press)

Jenkins, Steve (2004) *Hottest, Coldest, Highest, Deepest.* (Houghton-Mifflin)

— (2001) *What Do You Do When Something Wants to Eat You?* (Houghton-Mifflin)

— (1995) *Looking Down.* (Houghton-Mifflin)

Kerley, Barbara (2006)*A Cool Drink of Water* (National Geographic Children's Books) Lin, Grace & McKneally, Ranida (2006) *Our Seasons* (Charlesbridge)

McCarthy, Mary (2007)*A Closer Look* (Greenwillow)

Mondo Publishing (2008) *Let's Talk About It: Oral Language—Reading &Writing.*

Seeger, Laura Vaccaro (2007)*First The* (Roaring Brooks Press)

Serafini, Frank (2008) *Looking Closely Through the Forest* (Kids Can Press)

Simon, Seymour (2004) *Animals Nobody Loves* (Harper-Collins)

— SeeMORE series (Harper-Collins)

Strauss, Rochelle (2007) *One Well: The story of water on earth* (Kids Can Press)

Sullivan, Robert, (ed.) (2003) *100 Photographs That Changed the World* (Life)

Weber, Belinda (2006) *The Best Book of Nighttime Animals* (Kingfisher)

White, Matt (2001) *Endurance: Shipwreck and Survival on a Sea of Ice.* (Red Brick Learning)

Take Two Books series (WrightGroup/McGraw-Hill)

Professional Books

Allington, R.L. & Cunningham, P.M. (2006) *Classrooms That Work: They Can All Read and Write*. 4th Ed. Columbus, OH: Allyn & Bacon.

Anderson, R.C. & P. D. Pearson (1984) "A Schematic-Theoretic View of Basic Processes in Reading" In *Handbook of Reading Research*, ed. P.D. Pearson. New York, NY: Longman.

BC Ministry of Education (2006) *English Language Arts Integrated Resource Package K–7*.

Buhrow, Brad & Garcia, Anne Upczak (2007) *Ladybugs, Tornados, and Swirling Galaxies: English language learners discover their world through inquiry*. Portland, ME: Stenhouse.

Campbell, Brian & Fulton, Lori (2003) *Science Notebooks – Writing About Inquiry*. Portsmouth, NH: Heinemann.

Carson, Rachel (1998) *The Sense of Wonder*. New York, NY: Harper Collins.

Duke, Nell K. & Bennett-Armistead, Susan (2003) *Reading and Writing Informational Text in the Primary Grades*. New York, NY: Scholastic.

Dymock, Sue and Nicholson, Tom (2007) *Teaching Text Structures: A Key to Non-fiction Reading Success*. New York, NY: Scholastic.

Fielding, Linda & Pearson, P. David (1994) "Reading Comprehension: What Works?" *Educational Leadership* 51, 5: 62–67.

Gardner, J & Peters, C. (2005) *Whole Class Reading Assessment*. Vernon, BC: SD #22.

Harvey, Stephanie (1998) *Nonfiction Matters: Reading, writing, and research in grades 3–8*. Portland, ME: Stenhouse.

Harvey, Stephanie & Goudvis, Anne (2005) *The Comprehension Toolkit*. Portsmouth, NH: Heinemann.

— (2007) *Strategies that Work: Teaching comprehension to enhance understanding*. Portland, ME: Stenhouse.

— (2000) *Strategies That Work: Teaching Comprehension to Enhance Understanding* 1st Ed. Portland, ME: Stenhouse.

Hoyt, Linda (2002) *Making It Real: Strategies for success with informational texts*. Portsmouth, NH: Heinemann.

Jeroski, Sharon, Brownlie, Faye, & Kaser, Linda (1990) *Reading and Responding: Evaluation Resources for Your Classroom*. Toronto, ON: Nelson.

Keene E. & Zimmerman, S. (1997) *Mosaic of Thought, Second Edition: The Power of Comprehension Strategy Instruction* . Portsmouth, NH: Heinemann.

Kelley, Michelle & Clausen-Grace, Nicki (2007) *Comprehension Shouldn't Be Silent: From Strategy Instruction to Student Independence*. International Reading Association.

Manz, S.L. (2002) "A strategy for previewing textbooks: Teaching readers to become THIEVES" *The Reading Teacher*, 55, 434–435.

McGregor, Tanny (2007) *Comprehension Connections: Bridges to Strategic Reading*. Portsmouth, NH: Heinemann.

Miller, Debbie (2002) *Reading with Meaning: Teaching comprehension in the primary grades*. Portland, ME: Stenhouse.

Ontario Ministry of Education (2004) *Literacy for Learning: The Report of the expert panel on literacy in grades 4–6 in Ontario*.

Pearson, P. David & Gallagher, M.C. (1983) "The Instruction of Reading Comprehension" *Contemporary Educational Psychology* 8: 317–344.

Perkins, David (1993) *The Professional Journal of the American Federation of Teachers* v 17 n 3, pp. 8, 28–35, Fall 1993.

Peterson, R. & Asselstine, L. (2001) *Creating the Curious Classroom*. Toronto, ON: Harcourt.

Regie Routman (2003) *Reading Essentials: The Specifics You Need To Teach Reading Well*. Portsmouth, NH: Heinemann.

Scholastic Education (2008) *Moving Up with Literacy Place: A Complete Balanced Literacy Resource for Canadian Classrooms Gr. 4–6*. Toronto, ON: Scholastic Canada.

Shedd, John A. (1928) *Salt from My Attic* (self-published).

Stead, Tony (2002) *Is That a Fact? Teaching Nonfiction Writing K-3*. Portland, ME: Stenhouse.

— (2006) *Reality Checks: Teaching reading comprehension with nonfiction K–5*. Portland, ME: Stenhouse.

Sullivan, Robert, (ed.) (2003) *100 Photographs That Changed the World*. New York, NY: Life.

Wells, Jan & Reid, Janine (2004) *Writing Anchors*. Markham, ON: Pembroke.

Websites

www.readingatoz.com

www.readinglady.com

www.readingquest.org.

www.readwritethink.org

www.timeforkids.com

Index